Cambodia
Entering a New Phase of Growth

EDITOR
Olaf Unteroberdoerster

INTERNATIONAL MONETARY FUND

Cover design: IMF Multimedia Services Division

Cataloging-in-Publication Data
Joint Bank-Fund Library

Cambodia : entering a new phase of growth / editor, Olaf Unteroberdoester. — Washington, D.C. : International Monetary Fund, ©2014.
p. ; cm.

Includes bibliographical references and index.
ISBN: 978-1-47556-078-7

1. Cambodia—Economic conditions. 2. Economic development—Cambodia. 3. Finance—Cambodia. 4. Fiscal policy—Cambodia. I. Unteroberdoester, Olaf. II. International Monetary Fund.

HC422.C36 2014

Please send orders to:
International Monetary Fund, Publication Services
P.O. Box 92780, Washington, DC 20090, U.S.A.
Tel.: (202) 623-7430 Fax: (202) 623-7201
E-mail: publications@imf.org
Internet: www.elibrary.imf.org
www.imfbookstore.org

Contents

Preface

This study on Cambodia documents an economy at the crossroads and focuses on the main fiscal and financial sector challenges that Cambodian policymakers face as they chart a path to greater and shared prosperity. It draws on the findings of technical assistance reports and research papers prepared by IMF staff in the context of the IMF's annual Article IV consultations with Cambodia during 2010–12. Updates with respect to more recent data and developments are as of July 2013.

The study is the result of a group effort and was prepared by a team led by Olaf Unteroberdoerster and comprising Faisal Ahmed, Nombulelo Duma, Tubagus Feridhanusetyawan, Jung Yeon Kim, Rodolfo Maino, Phurichai Rungcharoenkitkul, Jookyung Ree, and Nujin Suphaphiphat. We thank David Cowen, numerous colleagues, and participants in seminars for helpful comments on earlier drafts of the chapters, and Rosanne Heller for editorial assistance. Sun Mi Lee and To-Nhu Dao provided valuable assistance in preparing the manuscript, and Joanne Johnson of the IMF Communications Department managed the editing and production of this publication.

CHAPTER 1

Introduction: Cambodia Entering a New Phase of Growth

OLAF UNTEROBERDOERSTER

Cambodia is about to leave behind its post-conflict status. Although the nation's efforts at rebuilding and recovery were initially beset with internal tensions and civil unrest, its hard-won macroeconomic stability and steady adherence to prudent policies gradually prevailed. This has allowed Cambodia to become one of the world's fastest-growing economies in the first decade of this century. As a result, progress in reducing poverty has been faster than in most other low-income countries, pushing Cambodia into the top five Millennium Development Goals trailblazers (Leo and Barmeier, 2010). The economic difficulties and policy challenges of the past 30 years of reconstruction—as well as the achievements—have been well documented, including in a 2006 IMF publication, *Cambodia: Rebuilding for a Challenging Future* (Coe and others, 2006).

This book focuses on the new challenges facing Cambodia's next generation. Our starting point is a Cambodia entering a new phase of rapid transformation and aspiring to become an emerging market economy. A testament to Cambodia's newfound vibrancy is its remarkable recovery from the global financial crisis of 2008–09. Since then, its garment exports have risen by more than two-thirds, led by robust retail sales in the United States and improved access to the European Union. Tourist arrivals have continued to grow at a brisk pace, while the recent sharp increase in construction approvals points to a rebound of the battered real estate sector and a return of investor confidence. In addition, early support for farmers' replanting efforts and improvements in rural infrastructure helped to lessen the severity of the impact of the floods in late 2011, which were the country's worst floods in a decade.

Yet as policymakers chart a path to enhanced development and shared prosperity, they will need to tackle Cambodia's main structural vulnerabilities, which were so painfully exposed when growth collapsed during the global crisis:

- ***A narrow economic base***: Exports have remained narrow-based, with garments and tourism accounting for more than 95 percent of foreign exchange earnings. At the same time, backward linkages of the manufacturing and services sectors to the rural economy—home to about 70 percent of Cambodia's poor—are still very limited.

- ***A dollarized and fragmented financial system***: Despite nearly two decades of low inflation, Cambodia's financial system is highly dollarized, limiting its scope for absorbing external shocks and increasing its banks' vulnerabilities to solvency and liquidity risks. Moreover, the banking system is both concentrated and fragmented, especially between urban and rural areas, posing risks to stability without adequate benefits for competition and innovation.
- ***Limited policy space***: The burden of macroeconomic management rests on fiscal policy. However, over the medium term, low fiscal revenues severely constrain the government's ability to address its development priority needs and raise investment in infrastructure and education, key drivers for future growth.

Part I of this book takes a closer look at these challenges and shows an economy at a crossroads. Chapter 2 offers a growth diagnostic, a framework to analyze the main drivers of Cambodia's future growth. It makes clear that for Cambodia to achieve a higher development trajectory, productivity growth will need to be unleashed by removing infrastructure bottlenecks, which in turn are holding back private investment, both domestic and foreign.

Chapters 3 and 4 move beyond the real economy and bring into focus the imbalances in Cambodia's financial development. The first imbalance stems from the fact that Cambodia is Asia's most dollarized economy. Somewhat paradoxically, growing dollarization in Cambodia has occurred against a backdrop of greater macroeconomic and political stability. The usual motive, currency substitution, does not appear to have been a factor. The dollarization instead reflects Cambodia's unbalanced and narrow growth so far, driven by its dollarized urban export and tourism sectors. Therefore, more diversified development with greater emphasis on agriculture and rural areas, where the riel is commonly accepted, could over time contribute to a significant decline in dollarization. In addition, Cambodia could try to create stronger incentives for the public use of riels by adapting the policies and experiences of other countries that have successfully dedollarized.

The second financial sector imbalance, examined in Chapter 4, concerns the paradox that Cambodia's still young financial system is already overbanked—that is, there are too many banks. This conclusion holds whether Cambodia is compared with its developmental peers, its regional neighbors, or even with countries that have much higher income levels and much larger and more well-developed financial systems. However, as the chapter highlights, the proliferation of banks not only stretches scarce supervisory resources but can also harm competition and financial stability, given the banking system's ownership structure and fragmentation. As a result, the chapter stresses the need for more stringent bank licensing and continued improvements in banking supervision, in both qualitative and quantitative terms.

Chapter 5, which concludes Part I, provides a comprehensive and integrated assessment of Cambodia's external, financial, and fiscal vulnerabilities. These are all linked to the unique features of Cambodia's post-conflict reform and growth experience. The vulnerability assessment takes stock not only of Cambodia's initial structural conditions and policy buffers but also of the vulnerabilities and emerging risks from changes in the external environment and the ongoing transformation in the domestic economy. Particular emphasis is given to the opportunities and challenges arising from the economic rebalancing taking place across Asia, in particular the emerging role of China. The chapter concludes by advocating a virtuous cycle of vulnerability-mitigating macroeconomic policies that could lay the foundations for high and sustained growth.

Part II of the book takes a more detailed look at these policies. Focusing on fiscal and financial sector policies, the common observation throughout this book is that greater policy buffers are needed to cushion adverse shocks in the near term and reduce structural vulnerabilities and constraints to growth over the medium term. First, the government's new revenue mobilization strategy will play a central role, since it offers the best chance for Cambodia to meet its development needs while safeguarding fiscal sustainability. Second, efforts to enhance the credibility and effectiveness of monetary policy and adopt better safeguards for a rapidly evolving financial system will also help promote economic resilience. While the book argues for such fiscal and financial sector policies, the resulting improvements in macroeconomic management will only enable a virtuous cycle of self-sustaining and inclusive growth if they are combined with steadfast structural reform. In particular, better governance and public service delivery to enhance the effectiveness of high-priority social and infrastructure investments will be critical both for poverty reduction and private-sector-led economic diversification.

The detailed policy challenges and recommendations provided in the chapters are summarized next.

CREATING AND SAFEGUARDING FISCAL SPACE

Cambodia currently has limited fiscal space. That is to say, the government has only a limited capacity for responding to adverse macroeconomic shocks and, over the medium term, for providing adequate resources to meet the country's vast development needs. The fiscal challenges are threefold: Cambodia needs to mobilize more revenue to rebuild fiscal space; it needs to better manage public debt to safeguard this space and ensure fiscal and debt sustainability; and it needs to strengthen public financial management to improve the quality, or effectiveness, of government spending.

In particular, Cambodia's capacity to collect tax revenue remains weak by international standards, depriving the government of critical resources to fund priority investments in infrastructure and social sectors. Moreover, there are important risks to fiscal sustainability because of the narrow tax base and the high correlation of the country's revenues with advanced economies' business cycle. Against this background, this book outlines the rationale for the government's new strategy to rebuild fiscal space by mobilizing domestic revenue.

A three-pronged approach is essential:

- improving revenue administration
- reforming tax policy to broaden the tax base and make revenues more buoyant, and
- strengthening governance.

Simultaneous implementation in these three reform areas is critical because progress in one area would create positive feedback to the others, making revenue mobilization more effective and self-sustaining. However, while greater revenue mobilization is the key to increasing fiscal space, careful management of fiscal risks and public expenditures is the key to safeguarding it. Therefore, this book also discusses ways to minimize the risks associated with rapidly growing contingent fiscal liabilities and ways to strengthen implementation of Cambodia's public financial management reform program.

TOWARD GREATER MONETARY INDEPENDENCE AND FINANCIAL DEVELOPMENT

In a low-income and heavily dollarized economy such as Cambodia's, policymakers face the dual challenge of striving to attain monetary policy independence (and dedollarize the economy) while ensuring steady progress in financial market development to support economic growth and broad economic development. The recent launch of the stock exchange and the issuance of negotiable certificates of deposit are two examples that show the dilemma that arises in pursuing these two objectives: Faster financial deepening based on investors' current currency preferences and market customs could cement the high degree of dollarization. To resolve this dilemma, the book proposes a strategic roadmap, highlighting two of its key elements. The first element is the right *sequencing* of policies needed to gradually achieve monetary policy independence and, ultimately, to establish a market-based monetary policy instrument in the Cambodian riel, without hindering progress in financial development. The second element is the right design of *incentives* that not only promote greater use of the riel but also provide a catalyst for a gradual convergence toward a market-based and independent monetary policy framework.

ENSURING A SOUND FINANCIAL SYSTEM

Attaining sustainable economic growth in Cambodia also requires a sound financial system. In addition to the stability risks discussed in Part I, the regulatory framework is currently marked by conflicts and overlaps, which interact with uneven implementation and enforcement of recently strengthened regulations. Cambodia's supervisory capacity is still limited, and a comprehensive crisis management framework is missing. Also missing is an adequate infrastructure to support the Cambodian Stock Exchange, including an adequate liquidity management framework and timely development of a foreign exchange market.

Notwithstanding these challenges, Cambodia has achieved a number of milestones in recent years and has made significant strides in establishing a legal and regulatory framework for financial sector activities. Based on the IMF-World Bank 2010 Financial Sector Assessment Program (FSAP) and relevant follow-up work, Part II of this book reviews in greater detail the milestones achieved in recent years and discusses key recommendations going forward in developing the financial sector. In particular, the analysis explores ways to strengthen the National Bank of Cambodia's financial supervision function commensurate with the development of a more complex financial system.

CONCLUSION

Cambodia's achievements over the last three decades have been remarkable. The nation is now set to join the new generation of Asia's frontier economies, aptly called Asia's "flying geese" by the Japanese economist Kaname Akamatsu in describing the rise of Asia's emerging markets since the middle of the 20th century. But the path to greater and more shared prosperity will require a solid foundation of sound macroeconomic policies. Creating and safeguarding fiscal space, enabling financial deepening while allowing the riel to play a greater role in the economy, and addressing financial stability challenges in a forward-looking manner—all are key elements of a virtuous cycle of sound macroeconomic policies and more resilient growth. Along with integrating its policy approach, Cambodia's transition to an emerging market economy will require modernizing the role of government and strengthening coordination among relevant government agencies during the formulation and implementation of those policies.

REFERENCES

Coe, D. T., I. Lee, W. F. Abdelati, D. Eastman, R. P. Hagemann, S. Ishikawa, A. Lopez-Mejia, S. Mitra, K. Nakamura, N. Rendak, S. Yelten, and S. Muñoz, 2006, *Cambodia: Rebuilding for a Challenging Future* (Washington: International Monetary Fund).

Leo, B., and J. Barmeier, 2010, "Who are the MDG Trailblazers? A New MDG Progress Index," Working Paper No. 222, Center for Global Development, Washington.

PART I

An Economy at a Crossroads

CHAPTER 2

How Fast Can Cambodia Grow? Assessing Key Drivers

PHURICHAI RUNGCHAROENKITKUL

Accurate estimates of potential growth have always been in high demand, in both advanced and developing economies. This is hardly surprising, since long-term growth is not only the core objective of development policy but also a key anchor of economic stability. However, applying standard quantitative methods to estimate potential output in developing economies is subject to severe limitations. In particular, poor data coverage and a lack of high-frequency economic indicators make the use of standard filtering techniques more difficult. Moreover, because developing economies are often in the process of important structural changes, any model that relies on stable macroeconomic/behavioral relationships can be a misleading guide to the future. Yet it is far from clear that a judgment-based estimate will necessarily be a better alternative.

This chapter's primary objective is to introduce a tractable quantitative framework to assess potential growth in a developing economy. The framework is based on a small dynamic macroeconomic model that, by design, economizes on both the data and behavioral assumption requirements and also allows the incorporation of external assumptions and judgment calls. We will show that the model can be used alongside a more qualitative "growth diagnostic" approach (introduced by Hausmann, Rodrik, and Velasco, 2005).

Cambodia's current macroeconomic backdrop makes it an especially interesting application of the proposed framework. The last decade was, for the most part, a fast-growing period for the country, with its economy expanding by 9.8 percent on average over 1999–2007, doubling its standard of living in the process. The impressive growth performance resulted from a confluence of favorable factors, including the expansion of international trade, sustained investment, and improvements in productivity. However, Cambodia is at an important crossroads. Its productivity growth is constrained by a lack of adequate infrastructure,

---

The author was an economist in the IMF Asia and Pacific Department when the initial draft of this book chapter was prepared. He would like to thank Enrique Aldaz-Carroll, Roberto Cardarelli, and Olaf Unteroberdoerster for their insightful comments. He is also grateful to Jaromir Benes for his helpful advice on the IRIS open-source toolbox for macroeconomic modeling and forecasting. This chapter was previously published as IMF Working Paper No. 12/96 (Rungcharoenkitkul, 2012).

notably in the electricity and power sectors, and this lack in turn is holding back investment. Overreliance on a narrow export market, notably the low-skilled garment industry, also means the external engine of its growth is approaching its limit, unless the export sector moves up the value chain or diversifies into other products. Cambodia's growth potential will hinge on whether the country can successfully overcome these challenges in the coming years.

To assess the outlook for potential growth in Cambodia, this chapter proposes (i) a quantitative framework that accounts for the dynamics of the fundamental drivers of growth and (ii) an analytical diagnostic of the constraints to growth. The two parts of this strategy complement each other, with the model informing the analysis of growth impediments and at the same time serving as a tool to assess different scenarios informed by the qualitative analysis.

The model proposed here is an integration of several standard methods, which may be grouped into two main categories: (i) the production function approach and (ii) the state space or statistical filtering approach. The first approach assumes an aggregate production function and estimates each of its components (factor inputs and total factor productivity). The approach works best in more advanced economies, where there are more data on factor inputs (such as capital stock, labor participation, hours worked, and utilization rates), as well as good proxies for total factor productivity. For example, the U.S. Congressional Budget Office and the EU Commission use this method to estimate the potential growth in the United States and the European Union, respectively (see CBO, 2001; and Roeger, 2006).[1]

One drawback of the production function method, given its bottom-up philosophy, is that it does not exploit other macroeconomic predictions that can be useful for inferring potential output. In particular, macroeconomic theory suggests that, if shocks are transitory, potential output should be close to the smoother trend of realized output. Moreover, according to the Phillips curve, potential output should be relatively low compared with actual output when inflation is accelerating.

The second category of estimates of potential growth attempts to exploit these macroeconomic relationships. Statistical filters that produce smoothed output series (such as the Hodrick-Prescott (HP) and bandpass filters) are the simplest example. A more structural example considers potential output as an unobserved variable within a structural macroeconomic model. An estimation procedure can then be performed to extract the sequence of potential output that is most consistent with the predicted relationship. For an example of this state space/filtering approach, see Benes and others (2010).

---

[1]The production function approach can be motivated via an explicit microfoundation, as is done by Willman (2002) in another EU application. For developing economies, a simplified and reduced form of the method may instead be implemented. For example, Epstein and Macchiarelli (2010), using the case of Poland, focus on identifying the trend labor input in the production function (i.e., the natural rate of employment).

Both approaches have advantages and drawbacks. The first method offers an appealing identification of the drivers of potential growth, which is useful for the analysis of growth impediments. However, it requires detailed, granular data, a condition rarely met for developing countries. The second method can economize on the amount of data required by using restrictions from economic theory. Traditionally, the filtering method is most often used to explain the cyclical fluctuations of output around the trend (that is, to assess the output gap), but it does not allow a structural explanation of the sources of long-run growth.

This chapter develops a hybrid model that combines the strengths of both traditional methods. A small-scale structural macro model is proposed; it has a supply-side production function and thus is capable of explaining the dynamics of growth drivers. The model has a state-space structure, where unobserved variables are estimated using a Kalman filter. This eases the burden on data requirements, since not all variables need to be observed. Finally, the model includes the demand-side equations, namely for the processes governing the output gap and the Phillips curve, enabling it to utilize information from macroeconomic theory as in the standard filtering method.

The chapter is organized as follows. First, the small structural macro model is laid out and estimated for Cambodia to project potential growth over the next decade. This serves as a platform to conduct quantitative growth simulations under different scenarios. We then proceed to identify factors that may be hindering growth by examining a number of criteria according to which Cambodia may have fallen behind other lower-income peers. This growth diagnostic is then used in combination with the growth model developed in the first part of the chapter to provide a quantitative assessment of the growth dividends should the identified growth impediments be removed.

ESTIMATING POTENTIAL GROWTH FROM A SMALL MACRO MODEL

The Model

The potential output $\overline{Y}_t$ is modeled as a simple Cobb-Douglas aggregate production function with a Hicks-neutral productivity term:

$$\overline{Y}_t = A_t K_t^{\alpha} L_t^{1-\alpha} \tag{1}$$

where A_t is the productivity level, K_t is the physical capital stock, L_t is the labor input, and $0 < \alpha < 1$. The potential output is therefore determined by the supply side of the economy, with available factor inputs and technology dictating how much output the economy can potentially produce.

The capital stock evolves as a function of an exogenous saving rate, S_t:

$$K_t = (1-\delta) K_{t-1} + s_t Y_t \tag{2}$$

where δ is the depreciation rate, and Y_t is the level of actual output. The saving rate is fixed at its realized historical values over the estimation sample, while its future values are pinned by an assumption as part of a forecasting scenario. Since the modeled economy is open, the saving rate S_t is identical to the rate of total investment, both domestic and foreign. Labor input is determined by the demographics, growing exponentially at a constant rate l:

$$\log L_t = l + \log L_{t-1} + \varepsilon_t^L \tag{3}$$

with a white-noise shock ε_t^L.

The productivity term A_t is an aggregate of three subcomponents:

$$A_t = AO_t AG_t^{b_G} AM_t^{b_M} \tag{4}$$

where AG_t, AM_t and AO_t represent productivity in the agricultural, manufacturing, and other sectors, respectively. The productivity in each sector is subject to disturbances, but is expected to grow exponentially at a constant rate:

$$\log AG_t = c_G + \log AG_{t-1} + \varepsilon_t^{AG} \tag{5}$$

$$\log AM_t = c_M + \log AM_{t-1} + \varepsilon_t^{AM} \tag{6}$$

$$\log AO_t = c_O + \log AO_{t-1} + \varepsilon_t^{AO} \tag{7}$$

Demand shocks can cause the actual output to deviate from its potential level. For instance, capital and labor may be underutilized during recessions, causing actual output to fall below its potential level. These exogenous shocks are assumed not to have a permanent effect on output, and thus the output gap—$gap_t \equiv \log(Y_t / \overline{Y}_t)$—narrows as the effect of shocks disappears. The demand-side equation can be summarized in a reduced form as

$$gap_t = \beta\, gap_{t-1} + \varepsilon_t^Y \tag{8}$$

with ε_t^Y being a white-noise demand shock.

Inflation dynamics depend on the output gap and are therefore conditional on actual output, revealing information about the potential output. Inflation π_t is assumed to follow a canonical Phillips curve with a white-noise disturbance:

$$\pi_t = \gamma \pi_{t-1} + (1-\gamma)(gap_t + \overline{\pi}) + \varepsilon_t^{\pi} \tag{9}$$

In other words, inflation rises with the output gap, moves with inertia, and is subject to supply shocks such as changes in energy and international food prices. In the long run, inflation converges to a constant $\overline{\pi}$.

Potential Growth Estimate

The solution to equations (1) through (9) is characterized by a balanced growth path, with the potential output driven by productivity growth and factor accumulation. The model has a state space structure, where a subset of variables is observed, while others can be estimated from Kalman filtering. The observed variables are annual output Y_t, inflation π_t, labor input L_t, investment rate S_t, output gap gap_t, agricultural productivity AG_t, and manufacturing productivity AM_t.[2] The full estimation period is 1986–2011, and any missing data points are treated as unobserved, to be recovered by the filter algorithm. Appendix Table A2.1 provides details of the data sources and available dates for each series.

The model is log-linearized, solved, and estimated by the Bayesian method.[3] In almost all cases, only loose priors about the parameter values are imposed to allow data ample room to speak, by setting large prior standard deviations and wide minimum-maximum bounds. Only in the case of a is the prior maximum value binding after the estimation. Detailed information on the parameter priors and estimation results are given in Appendix Table A2.2.

The estimated model is used to forecast all endogenous variables up to the year 2020. The baseline projection (Figure 2.1) assumes that Cambodia will be able to maintain investment at 20 percent of output in each year (similar to the 2000–10 average of 19.6 percent). The estimate for labor growth is 3 percent, whereas the estimate for productivity growth is 3 percent in the agricultural sector, 15 percent in the manufacturing sector, and 3 percent in other sectors. These growth assumptions are all close to their historical values.

Findings. The baseline estimate shows that potential growth has been declining gradually from the peak of 8.7 percent in 2004–05 but is expected to stabilize at around 7.5 percent from 2012 onward without further shocks, provided the investment rate remains at 20 percent (Figure 2.1). The estimated output gap is currently in negative territory, but it should gradually close as actual output growth catches up with potential growth.

The breakdown of potential growth into contributions from factor accumulation and productivity gain is shown in Figure 2.2. Growth in productivity contributes about 3 percent to potential growth on average and has been a relatively stable source of growth for Cambodia. Factor accumulation contributes about 4 percent to potential growth on average, with roughly equal contributions from capital and labor accumulation over 1987–2011. However, during 2000–07 a

---

[2]A past estimate of the output gap, strictly speaking, is not required for the estimate of potential output. It is included here to "train" the model to produce a smooth estimate of potential growth. If in the modeler's view, the latent potential growth can fluctuate meaningfully, then the HP-filtered gap can be dropped from the list of observed variables.

[3]The procedure is implemented using an open-source MATLAB specialized toolbox, IRIS, developed by Jaromir Benes. Available via the internet at http://code.google.com/p/iris-toolbox-project/.

Figure 2.1 Potential Growth Estimate, Cambodia, 1989–2020 *(Percent)*

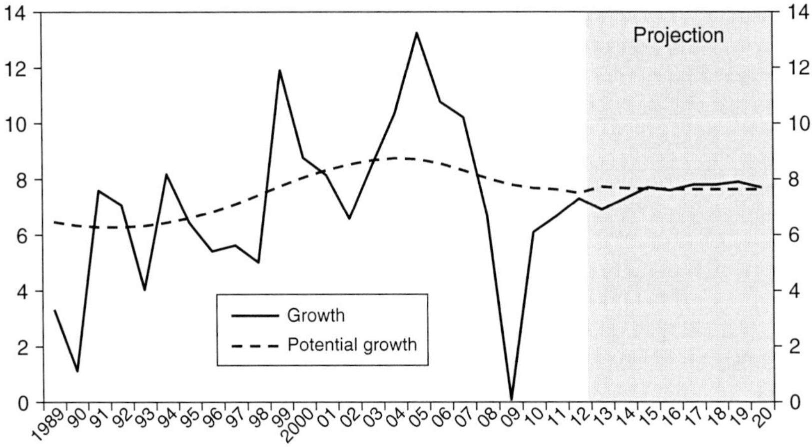

Sources: Data provided by the Cambodian authorities; and IMF staff estimates and projections.

Figure 2.2 Contributions to Past and Potential Growth, Cambodia, 1987–2020 *(Percent)*

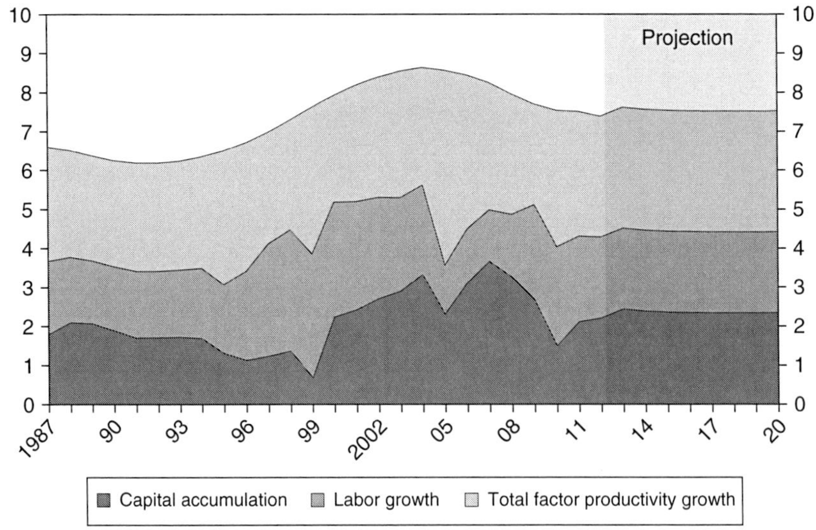

Sources: Data provided by the Cambodian authorities; and IMF staff estimates and projections.

rapid accumulation of capital stock contributed about 3 percent to growth and was a key driver of potential growth during this expansionary period. As factor accumulation slows going forward, growth is projected to moderate from the previous decade, supported for the most part by a continued gain in productivity, followed by sustained capital accumulation and labor growth.

Adverse Growth Scenarios

Clearly, if Cambodia fails to sustain its investment or productivity improvement, potential growth can be adversely affected. But by how much? Figure 2.3 compares the baseline potential growth with potential growth under two scenarios: (i) if the productivity in each sector grows at only half the rate as in the baseline, and (ii) if the investment-to-output ratio *St* is halved, relative to the baseline, to 10 percent.

Findings. A 50 percent reduction in productivity growth immediately reduces potential growth by over 1.5 percentage points and lowers potential growth permanently by 1.7 percentage points. On the other hand, a fall in the investment rate by half reduces potential growth by nearly 2 percentage points before sustained productivity gains (assumed to remain unchanged in this scenario) begin to lift potential growth. The boost from productivity only raises potential growth gradually, however, and the growth rate after 10 years still falls short of the baseline by more than 1 percentage point. In both cases, there will be substantial gaps between the *levels* of potential output compared with the baseline, and the gaps are still diverging after 10 years.

The possibility of highly nonlinear dynamics not captured by the model must be considered when using the model to analyze adverse scenarios. For a small open economy such as Cambodia's, there can be significant positive feedback between investment and productivity in ways not captured by the model. Higher productivity lowers production costs and raises profit margins, which helps attract foreign direct investment and accelerates capital accumulation. On the other hand, foreign investment brings technical know-how and is an important boost to productivity. Therefore, falling short of sustaining either investment or productivity may risk starting a vicious cycle of anemic growth.

Figure 2.3 Potential Growth Scenarios, Cambodia, 1987–2020 *(Percent)*

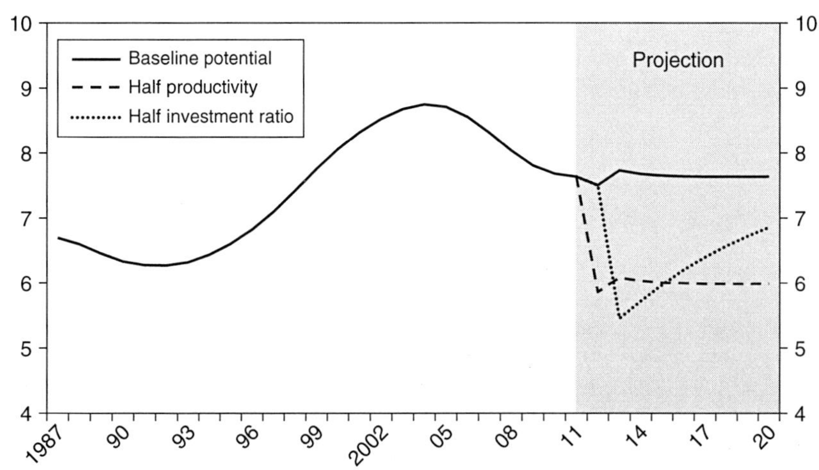

Sources: Data provided by the Cambodian authorities; and IMF staff estimates and projections.

What policy lessons can be drawn from the exercise so far? One clear policy priority is to continue to improve the quality of the factors of production by investing in education and labor skills. Another priority is to speed up the diffusion of technology to improve industrial efficiency. Third, investment in infrastructure to lower energy costs will also provide a significant boost to productivity, especially for the manufacturing sector.

The next step is to promote sectors that have greater room to benefit from productivity growth. In the manufacturing sector, this means moving up the value chain of the dominant garment industry or diversifying into other areas, such as electronics. The low-skilled garment industry has less room for productivity improvement, and its contribution to potential growth may inevitably decline in the longer term.[4]

GROWTH DIAGNOSTIC VIA CROSS-COUNTRY COMPARISON

What are the major growth-hindering factors in Cambodia? What can be done to alleviate these impediments and what is the likely effect on growth potential? This section aims to identify the constraints to growth drivers using a growth diagnostic exercise that relies on a cross-country comparison.[5] Impediments to growth drivers, namely investment and productivity, are then discussed in turn.

Identifying Impediments to Growth

Although investment has contributed significantly to Cambodian growth over the past decade, as a percentage of GDP investment in Cambodia remains among one of the lowest among low-income economies (Figure 2.4). A simple cross-country regression over 2000–09 shows that a 10 percent higher investment rate is associated with a 1.3 percent higher GDP growth rate.[6] Meanwhile, a simulation based on the above macro model suggests that a 10 percent increase in investment can raise potential growth immediately by as much as 2 percent and that the positive growth effect can persist even after a decade (see below on Quantifying Growth Dividends). Investment therefore holds significant untapped potential as a key driver of future growth for Cambodia.

---

[4]The link between productivity in the traded goods sector ("export sophistication") and economic growth is documented by Hausmann, Hwang, and Rodrick (2007). They also highlight the difficulties in transitioning from less to highly sophisticated markets without policy support, owing to the presence of network externalities.

[5]See Hausmann, Rodrick, and Velasco, 2005.

[6]The estimated cross-sectional equation is $y = 1.03 + 0.13x$ with $R^2 = 0.38$, where y denotes real GDP growth per capita averaged over 2000–2009, and x is the gross fixed capital formation as a percentage of GDP averaged over 2000–2009. The sample countries comprise Bangladesh, Bhutan, Cambodia, China, India, Indonesia, Lao P.D.R., Mongolia, Nepal, Pakistan, the Philippines, Sri Lanka, and Vietnam.

Figure 2.4 Average Investment-to-GDP, Selected Asian Economies, 2000–09 *(Percent)*

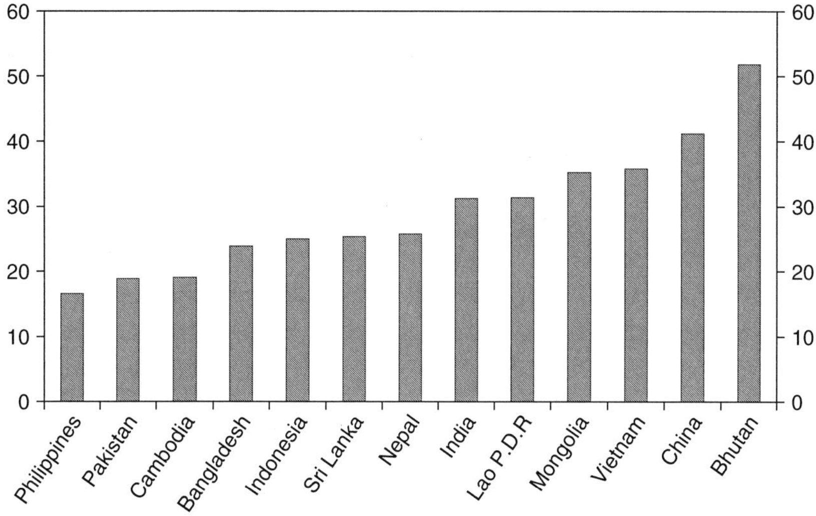

Sources: IMF World Economic Outlook database.

However, a combination of factors is currently holding investment back. Mitigating these constraints will be an important first step toward unleashing investment. According to the *Doing Business 2012* report by the World Bank and the International Finance Corporation, investors have found it harder to start a business, obtain a construction permit, and have contracts enforced in Cambodia than in many other countries. As Figure 2.5 illustrates, Cambodia ranks in 133rd place in overall ease of doing business, trailing most of its lower-income peers, and also scores poorly in the perception of corruption, according to Transparency International (see Chapter 3). Such rent seeking can deter private investment, cause a misallocation of resources that compromises investment efficiency, and ultimately hurt growth.

A lack of adequate infrastructure is also restraining investment, as well as hampering total factor productivity. As Figure 2.6 shows, Cambodia compares less favorably against its peers in basic indicators such as available telephone lines and Internet users. Meanwhile, prohibitively expensive power has been a binding obstacle for Cambodia, constraining power consumption per capita, which is currently low relative to other developing countries. Newly built hydropower plants will likely help ease some constraints on investment and growth, but they should be supplemented by wider measures to improve other basic infrastructure. There is robust evidence that factors such as the ease of doing business and basic infrastructure are important determinants of private investment in Asia (IMF, 2010).

Figure 2.5 Hindrance to Investment, Selected Asian Economies, 2012 *(International rankings)*

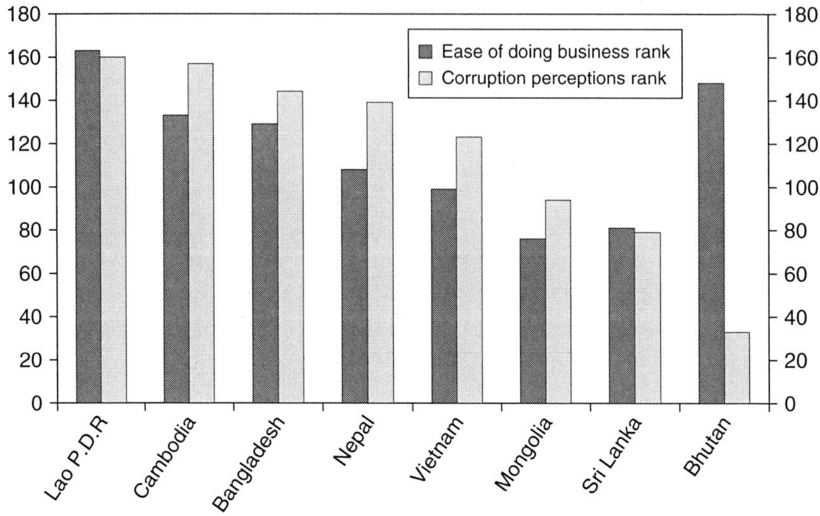

Sources: World Bank, *Doing Business*; and Transparency International, *Corruption Perceptions Index.*

Figure 2.6 Infrastructure, Selected Asian Economies, 2008/09

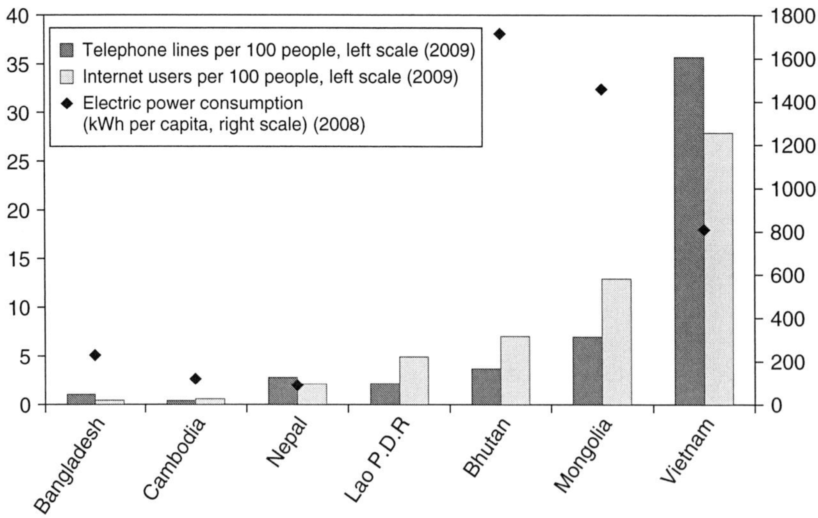

Source: World Bank, *World Development Indicators.*

Although productivity gains have been a key driver of Cambodia's growth, not all sectors have witnessed a surge in productivity. Growth in the agricultural sector, for example, has been helped by an expansion in total harvested area, whereas crop yields remain similar to those in the less productive competitors in the international market (Figure 2.7). As Cambodia's crop area inevitably stops expanding, and with its export market power still limited, its agricultural sector will need to rely on improvements in yield to continue growing and to increase global market competitiveness. Improving yield through greater use of physical capital such as machinery is one option, and it is another example of the complementary effects of investment and productivity.

Another important source of growth is labor productivity. The primary school enrollment rate was close to 90 percent in 2007. However, secondary school enrollment was much lower, at 34 percent, while the tertiary enrollment rate was only 5 percent. As the economy climbs up the technology ladder, the shortage of qualified labor will become an even more binding growth constraint. Therefore, an urgent need exists to speed up investment in human resources. However, public expenditure on education as a share of GDP in Cambodia is among the lowest compared to peers even after controlling for country-specific differences in level of development and educational attainment (Figure 2.8).

Although the manufacturing and export sectors have probably been major beneficiaries of productivity gains in the past, their exclusive reliance on a garment-led growth model may be more challenging going forward. While Cambodia has made efforts to diversify its export markets, the diversification in the product (as opposed to market) space is limited. As Figure 2.9 illustrates, the Herfindahl index of export diversification (in which a lower number indicates more diversification) has been higher for Cambodia than for many other Asian exporters. Countries such as China and Thailand, which have enjoyed a long period of sustained export-led growth, are highly diversified in the products that they export. Vietnam has also been diversifying. Only Bangladesh and Cambodia seem to have stalled in the progress toward greater diversification. The recent trend points toward less diversification in Cambodia, indicating

Figure 2.7 Cereal Yields, Selected Asian Economies, 2012

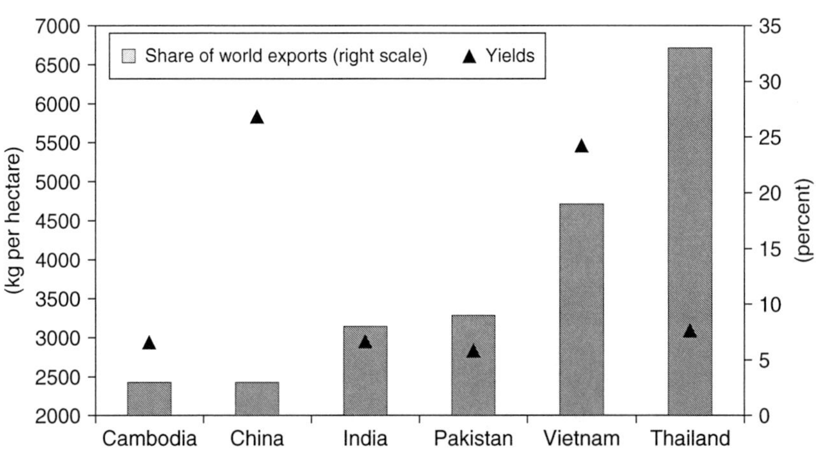

Source: World Bank, *World Development Indicators*.

Figure 2.8 Deviations from Predicted Public Spending on Education, Selected Asian Economies, 2011 *(In percent of GDP)*

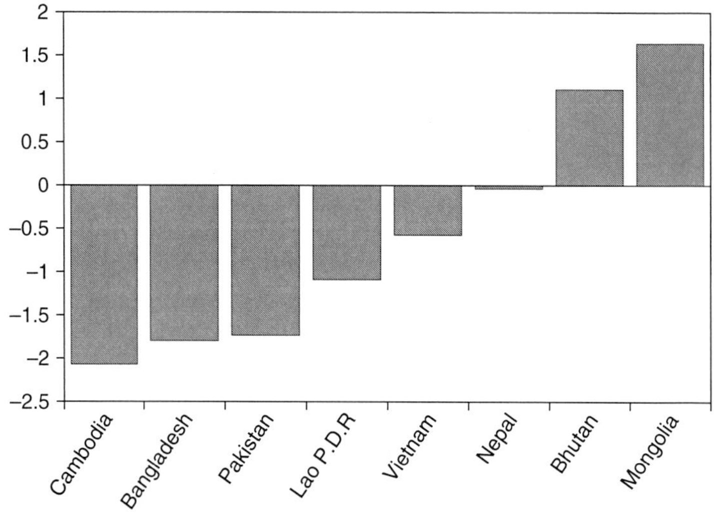

Source: IMF staff estimates.

Figure 2.9 Herfindahl Index of Export Diversification, Selected Asian Economies, 1980–2006

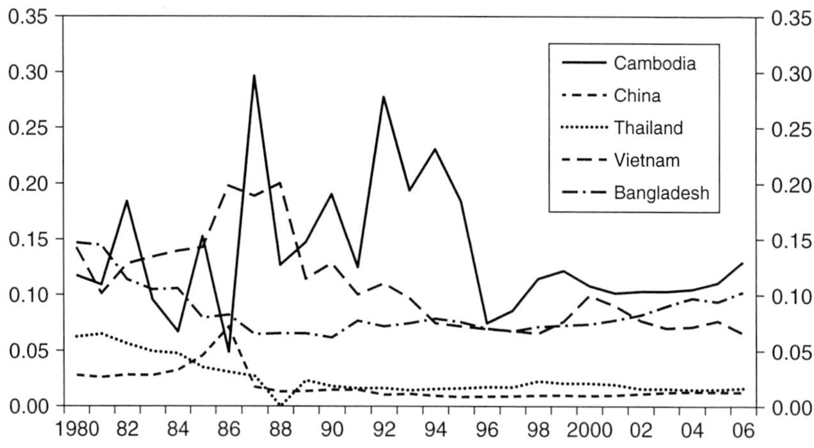

Source: World Bank, *Export Diversification Data*, PRMED.

that the country is following a different development path from a typical developing country.[7]

Conceptually, there are benefits and costs to both diversification and specialization, but in the case of Cambodia a number of factors currently point toward

[7]Imbs and Wacziarg (2003) document robust cross-country evidence that economies typically diversify until a certain income level is reached (typically around US$7,000–9,000 per capita), after which

increasing net benefits from export diversification. First, the uncertain global economic backdrop highlights the need for diversifying risks across both markets and products. Second, following years of rapid growth, Cambodia is now better positioned to start investing more in a wider range of sectors and promoting greater extensive margin trade.[8] Third, export diversification is an essential part of export discoveries, which in turn can lead to a renewed wave of productivity growth much needed by Cambodia. Finally, Cambodia's low labor costs and stable environment have started to attract foreign investors beyond the dominant garment sector, providing an opportunity to diversify its export industry into other areas of light manufacturing, such as car parts and electronics.

Pursuing greater export diversification will depend on the extent to which Cambodia succeeds in sustaining investment. Acemoglu and Zilibotti (1997) suggest that higher incomes make possible the diversification of indivisible risky projects. Consequently, countries should voluntarily choose to diversify more as their incomes grow, leading to a U-shaped pattern in sectoral concentration. The fact that Cambodia is not diversifying more rapidly may therefore be another symptom that investment is being hindered. Removing these constraints and related market failures not only will boost investment, which is an important engine for growth in itself, but will also lead to greater export discoveries and diversification, which will bring the fresh productivity gains that can be the backbone for sustained growth over the next decade.

In sum, despite Cambodia's strong record of growth in the past, the underlying fundamentals for its sustained growth on many fronts will need to be significantly strengthened before they are comparable to the standards of peers. To ensure robust growth over the longer term, therefore, structural reforms will be necessary to improve infrastructure and to promote investment and total factor productivity.

Quantifying Growth Dividends

How much additional growth could such structural reforms promote? Specifically, if the reforms were to succeed in bridging the gaps in infrastructure quality between Cambodia and its peers, how much would Cambodia's potential growth increase as a result? Estimates of investment elasticity to various measures of infrastructure quality have been computed by the IMF (2010) and are reproduced in the second column of Table 2.1. Gaps between the corresponding infrastructure quality of Cambodia and the average of its peers are shown in the first column; in all cases, the gaps are positive, indicating that Cambodia lags behind its peers. The calculation shows that

---

sectoral concentration resumes. Thus, the Herfindahl index typically decreases with income at an early stage of development, before rising later in a U-shaped pattern. Cambodia, on the other hand, has not followed this pattern and has not increased its diversification despite low per capita GDP (US$830 as of 2010).

[8]Extensive margin trade refers to increased exports of new products, which extends the frontier of exported product space. By contrast, intensive margin trade refers to growth in exports of existing products. Hummels and Klenow (2005) find that extensive margin trade accounts for around 60 percent of the export growth of advanced economies.

TABLE 2.1

Cambodia: Infrastructure Gaps and Investment

	Gap with peers	Investment elasticity	Extra investment rate (in percent of GDP)
Electric power consumption (kWh per capita)[a]	618	2.2	4.0
Telephone (lines per 100 persons)[b]	8	1.4	4.4
Paved roads (square meters per capita)[c]	0.5	4.0	4.8

Sources: World Bank. *World Development Indicators*; and IMF staff estimates.
[a]Based on 2008 data; peers comprise Bangladesh, Bhutan, Mongolia, Nepal, Timor-Leste, and Vietnam.
[b]Based on 2009 data; peers comprise Bangladesh, Bhutan, Lao P.D.R., Mongolia, Nepal, and Vietnam.
[c]Based on 2004 data; peer is Vietnam.

Figure 2.10 Potential Growth with Investment Boost, Cambodia, 1987–2020 *(Percent)*

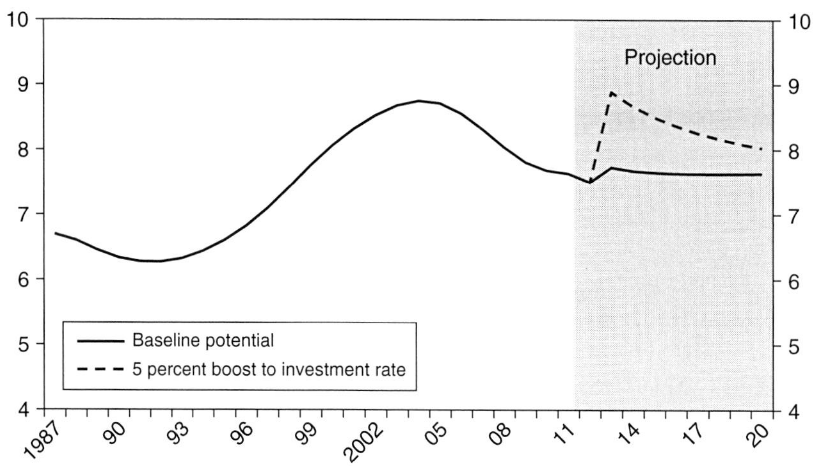

Sources: Data provided by the Cambodian authorities; and IMF staff estimates and projections.

if these gaps were to be closed by improved infrastructure, the estimated investment rate, shown in the third column, could be boosted by up to 5 percent of GDP.

In the event that the infrastructural improvements indeed raise the investment rate permanently by 5 percent of GDP, then the impact on potential growth based on the macro model would be as shown in Figure 2.10. The immediate effect on potential growth is about 1.2 percent, and the effect persists even after a decade. After 10 years, potential growth, despite declining from diminishing returns to physical capital, would still be 0.4 percentage point higher than without improvements in infrastructure. Thus, the growth impact is both substantial and long lasting. The cumulative effect of these growth dividends would lift the aggregate income level by more than 7 percent after 10 years.

This simulation does not capture the direct effect of infrastructural improvement on total factor productivity, nor the positive feedback between investment and productivity gains, both of which can be significant albeit harder to measure. At the same time, to the extent that structural reforms may have an adverse effect on some sectors (for example, cheaper electricity may render old production technology obsolete and lower the demand for low-skilled labor), the net effect on growth may also be smaller. Notwithstanding these interactional effects, the magnitude of growth dividends from improved infrastructure according to the model estimate is significant and likely to be of first-order importance.

CONCLUSION

A key advantage of the proposed framework is that the quantitative model complements the investigative approach (i.e., growth diagnostics, as adopted in this chapter) in important ways. The latter identifies key constraints to growth and potential sources of structural breaks, and thus closes the gap left by the model. The model can then be used to simulate the identified potential breaks in order to obtain a quantitative assessment that would otherwise be unavailable. Another advantage is that, since the model has a state space structure, the availability of data is of less concern, since missing or delayed data can be estimated by the filter.

Given these advantages, the framework can also be useful for other developing economies. The details of the model and the investigative research design are flexible and can be suitably adjusted to fit the country application. For example, for countries with more stable macro relationships, the model may be extended to include a Euler equation that endogenizes saving and investment. For countries with fully independent monetary policy, a policy rule can be added. If less is known about the sectoral productivities, modeling aggregate total factor productivity alone will suffice. As the growth diagnostic exercises differ from country to country, the model structure can also be tailored according to the focus of the analysis.

Regarding Cambodia's potential growth, the main findings are these: (i) Potential growth has indeed moderated from its 2004–05 peak, but the medium-term outlook of 7.5 percent remains relatively robust. (ii) However, the baseline outlook is conditional on Cambodia's ability to maintain its productivity growth and rate of investment, which are currently constrained by a number of structural impediments. (iii) Mitigating some of these impediments, for example by closing the infrastructural gaps between Cambodia and other developing peers, would translate into a significant boost to investment and a corresponding growth dividend.

APPENDIX

APPENDIX TABLE A2.1

Data for Observed Variables and Sources[1]

Variables	Data	Period covered	Sources
Y_t	Real GDP at 2000 prices	1986–2011	NIS, IMF
gap_t	Deviation of Y_t from the HP-filtered trend	1986–2011	NIS, IMF
π_t	CPI inflation (Phnom Penh)	1995–2011	NIS, IMF
L_t	Total labor force	1994–2009	WDI
S_t	Gross fixed capital formation to GDP	1995–2011	NIS, IMF
AG_t	Cereal yield (kg per hectare)	1994–2009	WDI
AM_t	Electricity production (kWh)	1995–2008	WDI

Note: CPI = consumer price index; HP = Hodrick-Prescott.

[1]National Institute of Statistics of Cambodia (NIS); and World Bank, *World Development Indicators* (WDI) 2011.

APPENDIX TABLE A2.2

Priors and Posterior Estimates of Parameters

	Prior		Posterior	
Parameters	Mode	Dispersion	Mode	Dispersion
α	0.2	0.9	0.3	NA
b_G	0.05	0.9	0.042	0.0002
b_M	0.05	0.9	0.013	0.0005
c_G	0.03	0.9	0.033	0.0004
c_M	0.03	0.9	0.150	0.0003
c_O	0.03	0.9	0.027	0.0000
δ	0.05	0.9	0.078	0.0006
β	0.9	0.9	0.494	0.0279
γ	0.9	0.9	0.424	0.0346
$\overline{\pi}$	0.07	0.5	0.061	0.0003
l_g	0.03	0.5	0.029	0.0000
$\sigma_{\varepsilon AG}$	0.01	0.9	0.099	1.8437
$\sigma_{\varepsilon AM}$	0.01	0.9	0.073	0.9984
$\sigma_{\varepsilon AO}$	0.01	0.9	0.006	0.0068
$\sigma_{\varepsilon L}$	0.01	0.9	0.011	0.0236
$\sigma_{\varepsilon Y}$	0.01	0.9	0.040	0.3100
$\sigma_{\varepsilon \pi}$	0.01	0.9	0.053	0.5314
$\sigma_{\varepsilon S}$	0.001	0.9	0.042	0.3365

Note: NA = not applicable.

REFERENCES

Acemoglu, D., and F. Zilibotti, 1997, "Was Prometheus Unbound by Chance? Risk, Diversification and Growth," *Journal of Political Economy*, Vol. 105, No. 4, pp. 709–51.

Benes, J., K. Clinton, R. Garcia-Saltos, M. Johnson, D. Laxton, P. Manchev, and T. Matheson, 2010, "Estimating Potential Output with a Multivariate Filter," IMF Working Paper No. 10/285 (Washington: International Monetary Fund).

Congressional Budget Office (CBO), 2001, "CBO's Method for Estimating Potential Output: An Update," http://www.cbo.gov/ftpdocs/30xx/doc3020/PotentialOutput.pdf.

Epstein, N., and C. Macchiarelli, 2010, "Estimating Poland's Potential Output: A Production Function Approach," Working Paper No. 10/15 (Washington: International Monetary Fund).

Hausmann, R., J. Hwang, and D. Rodrik, 2007, "What You Export Matters," *Journal of Economic Growth*, Vol. 12, No. 1, pp. 1–25.

Hausmann, R., D. Rodrik, and A. Velasco, 2005, "Growth Diagnostics" (Cambridge, MA: John F. Kennedy School of Government, Harvard University Center for International Development).

Hummels, D., and P. J. Klenow, 2005, "The Variety and Quality of a Nation's Exports," *American Economic Review*, Vol. 95, No. 3, pp. 704–23.

Imbs, J., and R. Wacziarg, 2003, "Stages of Diversification," *American Economic Review*, Vol. 93, No. 1, pp. 63–86.

International Monetary Fund (IMF), 2010, "Investment and Rebalancing in Asia," *Regional Economic Outlook: Asia and Pacific* (October), pp. 57–70.

Roeger, W., 2006, "The Production Function Approach to Calculating Potential Growth and Output Gaps: Estimates for EU Member States and the US," EU Commission, DG ECFIN.

Rungcharoenkitkul, Phurichai, 2012, "Modeling with Limited Data: Estimating Potential Growth in Cambodia," IMF Working Paper No. 12/96 (Washington: International Monetary Fund).

Willman, A., 2002, "Euro Area Production Function and Potential Output: A Supply Side System Approach," Working Paper No. 153 (Frankfurt: European Central Bank).

CHAPTER 3

Asia's Most Dollarized Economy: Causes and Consequences

NOMBULELO DUMA

Cambodia has made great strides toward macroeconomic and political stability over the past decade. Following decades of civil war and the Khmer Rouge regime, reconstruction efforts began in the mid-1990s. The establishment of peace in 1991 was followed by sizable foreign donor aid and a rebuilding of human capital, physical infrastructure, and institutions (Coe and others, 2006). Significant dollar inflows have contributed to strong economic growth, which during 2000–11 surpassed that of other low-income countries in Asia (Figure 3.1). Per capita income has doubled over the past 10 years; inflation has, on average, been maintained in the single digits; and the incidence of poverty and rates of malnutrition have both fallen.

However, dollarization has continued to rise. Measured as the ratio of foreign currency deposits to broad money, dollarization has risen from about 60 percent in the late 1990s to over 80 percent in 2012 (Figure 3.1). Cambodia is classified as partially dollarized, meaning that the U.S. dollar circulates in conjunction with its official national currency—the riel—as opposed to being fully dollarized, as in economies where the dollar is the only legal tender. In contrast with Cambodia, in comparable partially dollarized low-income countries in Asia dollarization has either declined or remained much lower over the same period. In Lao P.D.R., dollarization has declined from around 80 percent in the early 2000s to less than 50 percent in recent years. Dollarization is just above 30 percent in Mongolia and below 20 percent in Vietnam. The increase in dollarization in Cambodia has been contrary to the general belief that macroeconomic and political stability help reduce dollarization.

This chapter explores the factors that have contributed to Cambodia's dollarization and reviews lessons from international experience to help devise strategies for de-dollarization. After a general discussion of the causes of dollarization, the chapter reviews the Cambodian experience with dollarization, including an econometric analysis of the extent to which changes in the U.S. federal funds rate affect Cambodia's macroeconomic aggregates. This is followed by lessons from successful dollarization cases. The chapter concludes with suggestions for increasing the use of the riel in Cambodia.

An earlier version of this chapter was published as IMF Working Paper No. 11/49 (Duma, 2011).

Figure 3.1

GDP growth (average, 2000–11)
(Annual average, percent change)

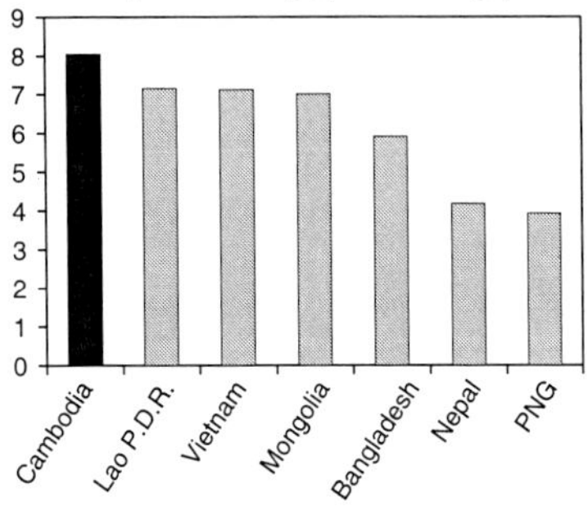

Sources: Data provided by authorities; and IMF staff estimates.

Per capita GDP (PPP), 2000 and 2011
(In U.S. dollar)

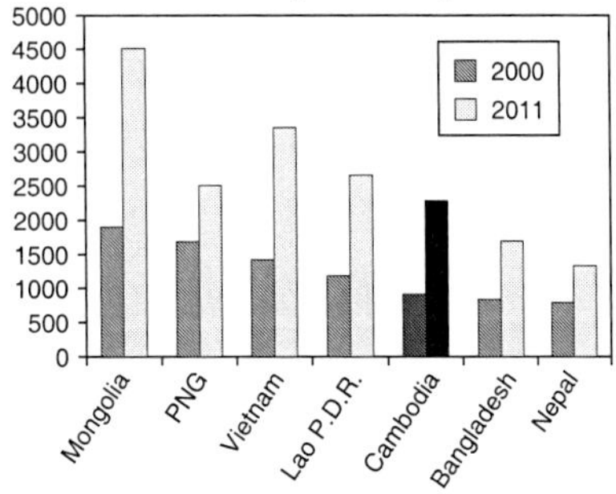

Source: IMF's World Economic Outlook.

Inflation (average, 2000–11)
(Annual average, percent change)

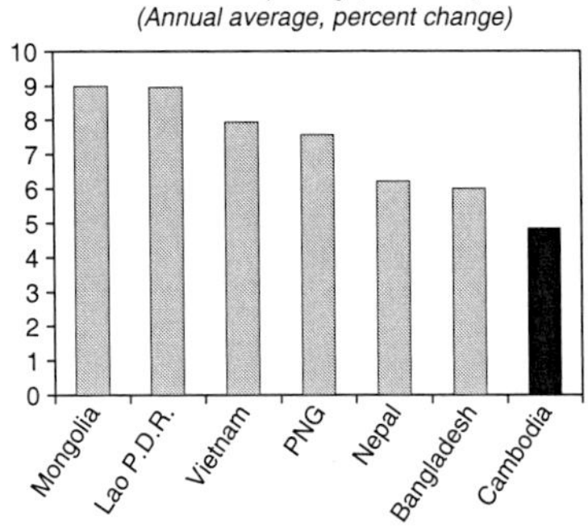

Sources: Data provided by authorities; and IMF staff estimates.

Ratio of foreign currency deposits to broad money, 2000–12
(In percent)

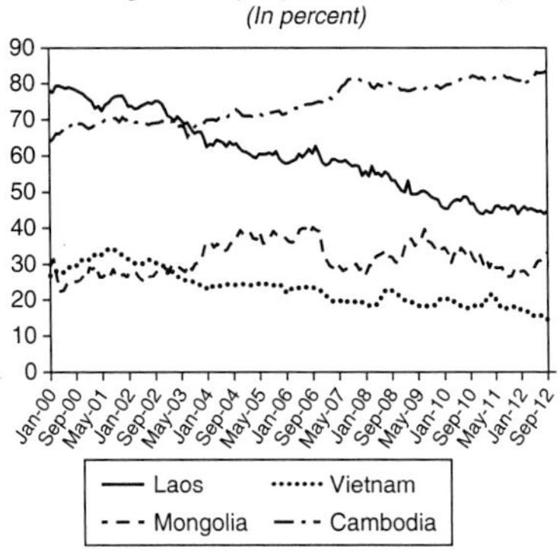

Sources: Data provided by the authorities; and IMF staff estimates.

Poverty headcount ratio at national poverty line
(Percent of population)

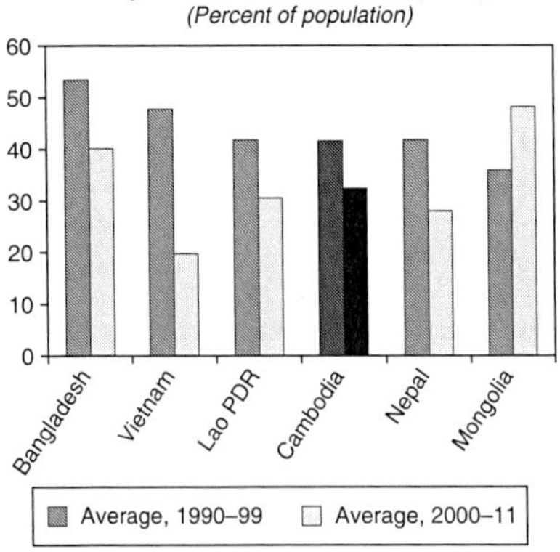

Source: World Bank database, *World Development Indicators;* and IMF staff estimates.

Malnutrition prevalence, weight for age[a]
(Percent of children under 5)

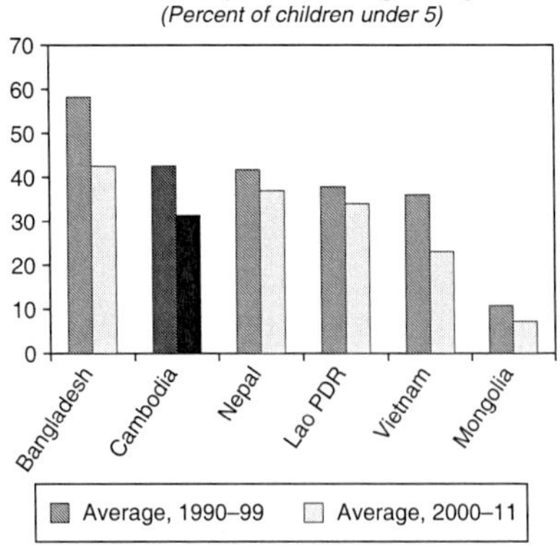

Sources: World Bank, *World Development Indicators;* and IMF staff estimates.

[a]Percentage of children under age 5 whose weight for ago is more than two standard deviations below the median for the international reference population ages 0–59 months.

DOLLARIZATION IN GENERAL

The macroeconomic literature identifies several possible causes of dollarization:

- *Large macroeconomic imbalances and hyperinflation*: Chile, Colombia, and Peru became dollarized following periods of macroeconomic instability and high inflation that resulted in the substitution of the U.S. dollar for their respective domestic currencies (Galindo and Leiderman, 2005; Herrera and Valdés, 2005; Kokenyne, Ley, and Veyrune, 2010; and Reinhart, Rogoff, and Savastano, 2003).
- *Financial repression and capital controls*: Nigeria, Venezuela, and many sub-Saharan African countries became dollarized following the introduction of policies that repressed financial transactions and imposed capital controls (Reinhart, Rogoff, and Savastano, 2003).
- *The appeal of the U.S. dollar as an anchor of macroeconomic stability*: Argentina and Ecuador adopted the U.S. dollar as legal tender, in Argentina's case to help address its long history of problems with monetary and exchange rate policies, and in Ecuador's case following a deep economic and political crisis (Berg and Borensztein, 2000).

Further, the literature has identified two main motives for the demand for foreign currency assets. The first is currency substitution, which is the use of foreign assets as a means of payment and a unit of account. Currency substitution tends to follow periods of hyperinflation, prompting the public to seek the use of alternative currencies. The second is asset substitution, which results from risk and return considerations between domestic and foreign assets. Price instability and prolonged depressions have prompted the use of foreign-currency-denominated assets as a store of value.

Once entrenched, dollarization is difficult to eliminate. Public memory of macroeconomic instability and hyperinflation tends to remain for a long time, resulting in the maintenance of foreign-currency-denominated assets even during periods of macroeconomic stability. The literature indicates that dollarization remains or does not subside entirely even when both macroeconomic stability and the credibility of government policies have been achieved (Kokenyne, Ley, and Veyrune, 2010).

THE CAMBODIAN EXPERIENCE WITH DOLLARIZATION

The use of dollars in Cambodia has come a long way. During the regime of the Khmer Rouge (1975–79), all barter, private commercial activity, private ownership, means of exchange, and stores of value were prohibited and punishable by death (Prasso, 2001). Savings and property were lost, and cash holdings were made worthless. Between 1975 and 1980, Cambodia was without a monetary system and without money. When the Cambodian riel was reintroduced in 1980, the experience during the Khmer Rouge period contributed to its low acceptance by the public, which instead, preferred other stores of value and means of payment, such as the U.S. dollar, gold, and even rice. Earlier, even the Vietnam dong and Thai baht had been widely used, but their use declined over time and became limited to the border areas with the respective countries.

With the passage of time, the use of the riel increased, and it is widely accepted in rural areas. Banking system riel deposits have grown sixfold since the mid-2000s, and one of the commercial banks engaged in microfinance has the majority of its loan portfolio denominated in riels in rural areas. Nevertheless, although the riel has increased in volume over recent years (Figure 3.2), dollar inflows have been larger. This indicates that the rise in dollarization from 2000 to 2012 has not necessarily come about through a substitution of riels for dollars but through a strong inflow of dollars, as also noted by Menon (2008). Although the ratio of riel deposits to GDP has risen, it remains at only around 1 percent of GDP. This compares with about 70 percent of GDP in Vietnam for dong deposits and about 8½ percent of GDP in Lao P.D.R. for kip deposits. Financial intermediation in riels remains low, partly reflecting constraints on access to finance in rural areas.

Growth in Cambodia's dollar economy has far surpassed that in its riel economy. Cambodia's economy has two parallel worlds: (i) an urban economy, which is mostly dollar based and has greatly benefited from the buoyant garments sector, tourism, foreign direct investment, and aid; and (ii) a rural economy, which is largely agricultural and is riel based. The contribution of the garment and tourism sectors has surpassed that of the agricultural sector (Figure 3.3). Significant inflows of aid, foreign direct investment, and tourism receipts, along with the growth of the garment export sector, which transacts in dollars—since the mid-1990s—have all contributed to the large amount of dollars.

Figure 3.2

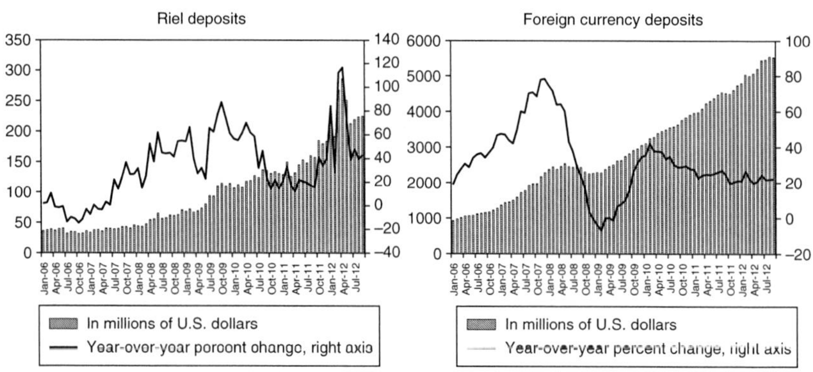

Sources: Data provided by the Cambodian authorities; and IMF staff estimates.

Figure 3.3

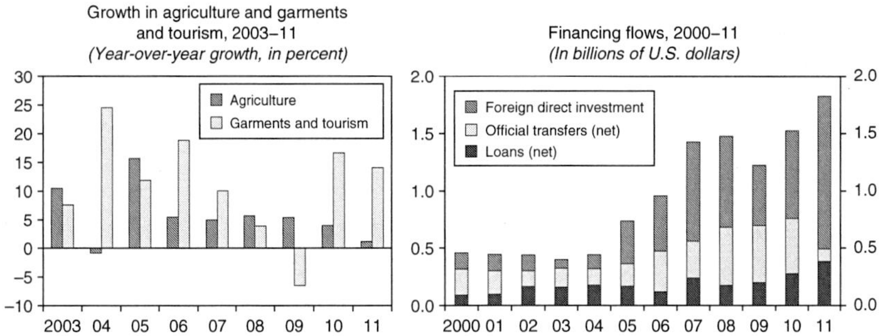

Sources: Data provided by the Cambodian authorities; and IMF staff estimates.

Costs and Risks of Dollarization

Limited influence over domestic monetary conditions. The National Bank of Cambodia (NBC) lacks instruments to influence monetary aggregates and anchor private sector expectations of inflation. Movements in private sector credit tend to be outside the control of the NBC. The extent of dollarization means the NBC effectively delegates its monetary policy to the United States. As illustrated in the next section and in the appendix to this chapter, macroeconomic variables in Cambodia respond significantly to changes in U.S. monetary policy. While the NBC occasionally uses the dollar reserve requirement ratio as a monetary policy tool to control liquidity, its effectiveness has proven to be limited.[1] When the reserve requirement ratio was reduced in early 2009 to provide liquidity to banks and to help boost economic activity in the wake of the global financial crisis, banks instead accumulated more reserves at the NBC. Excess reserves rose to their highest levels in history and credit to the private sector contracted.

Loss of seigniorage. Dollarization has resulted in the loss of seigniorage revenue. Seigniorage revenue is the difference between the value of money and the cost to produce it. When the cost of producing money exceeds (or is below) its value, seigniorage is negative (or positive). The cost of seigniorage can be estimated as a one-time stock cost from the amount of new foreign currency that is being acquired, or as a continuing flow cost in terms of seigniorage revenue foregone (Bogetić, 2000). Given the nature of dollarization in Cambodia and the way it occurred—that it was not a conscious official choice to adopt the dollar—the calculation of seigniorage loss using the continuing flow method is more appropriate. Through the creation of base money, the NBC buys real resources for

[1]Banks are required to hold reserves in U.S. dollars (for foreign currency deposits) and in riels (for riel deposits). As of end-2012, the required reserve ratio on foreign currency was 12.5 percent, while that on riel deposits was 8 percent. Required reserves are remunerated at one-half the Singapore interbank offered rate (SIBOR).

nothing in return—considering the cost of printing money and any remuneration of bank reserves by the monetary authorities. The high level of dollarization means the NBC forgoes this flow of revenue.

Because there is no measure of dollars in circulation in Cambodia, estimates of currency in circulation in comparator low-income countries in Asia (Mongolia, Nepal, and Vietnam)[2] are used as a proxy. The measure of the cost of dollarization is the outstanding amount of dollars in circulation multiplied by the dollar market interest rates in annual percent, as quoted in the United States. The interest rates considered are the federal funds rate, the prime lending rate, and the three-month Treasury bill rate; the results derived from using these interest rates are similar. The methodology helps determine lost income that can be recovered if dollars circulating in Cambodia are replaced with the riel to the level found in the comparator countries. Based on this proxy method, the seigniorage loss for Cambodia is estimated at up to 0.6 percent of GDP, based on estimates of currency in circulation for Vietnam as a proxy (Table 3.1). This estimate is significant when compared with Cambodia's small public revenue base (about 12½ percent of GDP, excluding grants).

Broader ranges of seigniorage estimates have been found in other countries. Bogetić (2000) estimated seigniorage loss for Latin American countries to range from ½ percent of GDP in Argentina to about 7½ percent of GDP in Ecuador for the period 1991–97. Similarly, Humpage (2002) estimated seigniorage loss for Latin American countries to range from 0.1 percent of GDP in Ecuador to about 5½ percent of GDP in Chile for the period 1990–2000.

Estimates of seigniorage loss should be interpreted with caution. The costs of dollarization in terms of seigniorage loss are very relevant when the government in question has or would have implemented optimal macroeconomic policies. Chang (2000) argues that, in cases where policy credibility has been a problem, interpreting seigniorage becomes more complicated. In countries in which dollarization has increased, the credibility of policies had been an issue. In these cases, the increase in dollarization could, in fact, have been associated with an increase in social welfare provided, which would otherwise not have occurred. Chang (2000) further argues that computed seigniorage loss can only be unambiguously interpreted as "real loss" to the economy if policy credibility problems are assumed away. In this light, dollarization has benefits, which have been evident in the stability of the Cambodian macroeconomy and in the containment of inflation. These benefits—while not necessarily quantifiable—have to be weighed against the costs.

Liquidity risk and limited lender of last resort. Sudden changes in investors' and depositors' perceptions of the health of the banking system, which result in a run on deposits, could compromise the NBC's international reserves. Therefore, high dollarization requires that the NBC maintain an adequate level of dollar

---

[2]Bangladesh and Lao P.D.R. were also assessed, but this produced insignificant results given that both countries have low levels of currency in circulation.

TABLE 3.1

Seigniorage Loss Estimates Based on Currency in Circulation in Comparator Low-Income Countries in Asia, 2007–11

		2007	2008	2009	2010	2011	Average 2007–11[a]
(1)	Currency in circulation in Asian low-income countries (In percent of GDP)						
	Mongolia	5.7	5.0	4.3	4.6	4.7	4.9
	Nepal	12.2	13.5	13.6	11.9	13.4	12.9
	Vietnam	19.3	15.9	17.7	17.1	14.6	16.9
(2) = ((1)*(8))/100	Proxy for Cambodia given its GDP:						
	Mongolia	493.8	519.1	450.3	521.0	603.8	517.6
	Nepal	1050.1	1402.2	1416.2	1341.8	1733.6	1388.8
	Vietnam	1665.7	1651.0	1841.4	1920.1	1886.5	1792.9
(3) = (2) – (9)	Deduct riels in circulation in Cambodia[b]						
	Mongolia	3.3	–46.9	–274.8	–219.4	–328.4	–173.3
	Nepal	559.5	836.2	691.0	601.4	801.5	697.9
	Vietnam	1175.1	1085.0	1116.2	1179.7	954.3	1102.1
	Seigniorage based on:						
(4) = (((3)*((10)/100))/(8))*100	U.S. federal funds rate						
	Mongolia	0.0	0.0	0.0	0.0	0.0	–0.1
	Nepal	0.3	0.2	0.0	0.0	0.0	0.3
	Vietnam	0.7	0.2	0.0	0.0	0.0	0.4
(5) = (((3)*((11)/100))/(8))*100	U.S. bank prime lending rate						
	Mongolia	0.0	0.0	–0.1	–0.1	–0.1	–0.1
	Nepal	0.5	0.4	0.2	0.2	0.2	0.5
	Vietnam	1.1	0.5	0.3	0.3	0.2	0.8

(Continued)

TABLE 3.1 ***(Continued)***

		2007	2008	2009	2010	2011	Average 2007–11[a]
(6) = (((3)*((12)/100))/(8))*100	U.S. 3-month Treasury bills rate[c]						
	Mongolia	0.0	0.0	0.0	0.0	0.0	−0.1
	Nepal	0.3	0.1	0.0	0.0	0.0	0.3
	Vietnam	0.6	0.1	0.0	0.0	0.0	0.4
(7) = average((4), (5), (6))	Seignorage loss estimate						
	Mongolia	0.0	0.0	0.0	0.0	0.0	−0.1
	Nepal	0.4	0.2	0.1	0.1	0.1	0.4
	Vietnam	0.8	0.3	0.1	0.1	0.1	0.6
	Memorandum items						
(8)	Nominal GDP (in millions of U.S. dollars)	8639.2	10351.9	10414.2	11255.1	12890.3	8594.6
(9)	Cambodia riels in circulation (in millions of U.S. dollars)	490.5	566.0	725.1	740.4	932.2	497.0
	(In percent of GDP)	5.7	5.5	7.0	6.6	7.2	5.8
(10)	U.S. federal funds rate	5.0	1.9	0.2	0.2	0.1	3.5
(11)	U.S. bank prime lending rate	8.1	5.1	3.3	3.3	3.3	6.5
(12)	U.S. 3-month Treasury bills rate	4.4	1.4	0.2	0.1	0.1	3.2

Source: U.S. Federal Reserve; author's calculations; and IMF staff estimates

[a]The average for interest rates is over a longer period of 1991–2011 to make it less biased toward the more recent low interest rates.

[b]During 2009–11, the amount of riels in circulation in Cambodia surpassed the amount of local currency circulating in Mongolia.

[c]A 6-month Treasury bills rate produced similar results.

liquidity both at the macro level (Figure 3.4) and at the individual financial institution level. However, although international reserves serve as the main backstop in the event of a severe banking system liquidity shortage in Cambodia, the coverage of foreign currency deposits by gross official reserves has declined over time.

Bank balance sheet risks. Balance sheet risks tend to arise in cases of partial dollarization. Dollarization tends to add to the banking sector vulnerabilities that arise from currency mismatches, exchange rate and credit risks, and dollar-denominated nonperforming loans (Unteroberdoerster, 2002). These vulnerabilities may be heightened because of direct exchange rate risks that result from currency mismatches in banks' balance sheets. Indirect credit risk may arise in the case of devaluations in the presence of substantial dollar lending to nonhedged borrowers (Kokenyne, Ley, and Veyrune, 2010).

Monetary Policy in Dollarized Cambodia

The extent of dollarization makes Cambodia susceptible to changes in U.S. monetary policy. This poses constraints on the domestically available tools with which to respond to external shocks. Monetary expansion in the United States tends to result in economic booms in other countries (Kim, 2001), including in dollarized economies (Goux and Cordahi, 2007). During late 2007 and early 2008, Cambodia experienced an increase in inflationary pressures as commodity prices and foreign inflows rose. Coincidentally, U.S. monetary policy had become loose following the Federal Reserve's attempt to increase liquidity as the subprime crisis hit. The federal funds rate had declined from about 5.26 percent in July 2007 to 1.98 percent by May 2008.

The high degree of dollarization raises the question of the extent to which Cambodia imports U.S. monetary policy. The fact that about 60 percent of

Figure 3.4

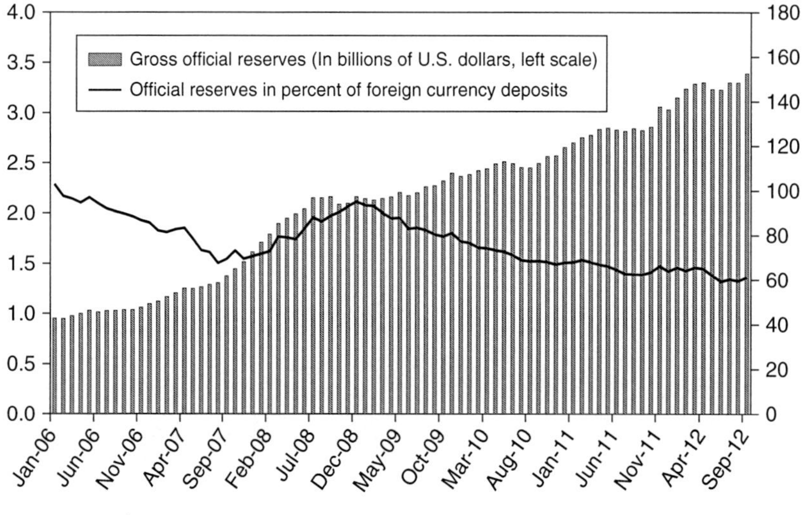

Cambodia's garment exports go to the United States indicates strong real linkages between the Cambodian economy and the U.S. economy in addition to the financial linkages caused by dollarization. The appendix to this chapter provides an analysis of the extent to which changes in the federal funds rate influence macroeconomic variables in Cambodia. The analysis finds that financial sector variables (including domestic interest rates) and real economy variables (including trade) respond greatly to changes in the federal funds rate within the first few months. A one standard deviation shock to the federal funds rate (an increase of about 0.3 percent) results in an increase in the lending rates of about 0.4 percent and in the deposit rates of about 0.5 percent as local banks attempt to minimize the spread between domestic and foreign interest rates. This illustrates the extent to which monetary conditions are beyond the control of the NBC.

Structural Challenges that Instill Dollarization

While Cambodia's economic growth track record has been impressive, several structural weaknesses inhibit faster economic development and private sector performance. Rennhack and Nozaki (2006) argue that weak institutions under-

Figure 3.5*

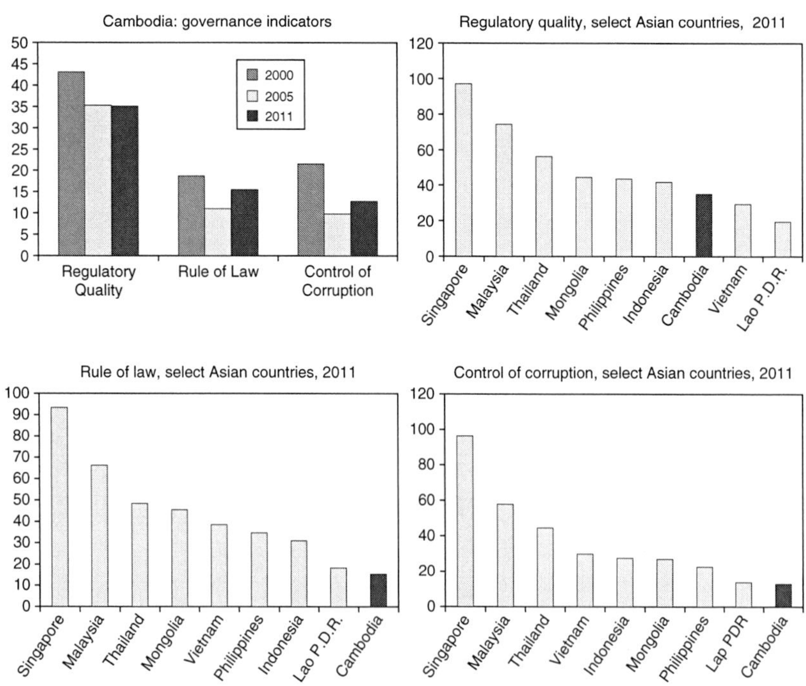

Source: World Bank, *World Governance Indicators.*

* Percentile rank indicates the percentage of countries worldwide that rate below the selected country. Higher values indicate better governance ratings.

Figure 3.6

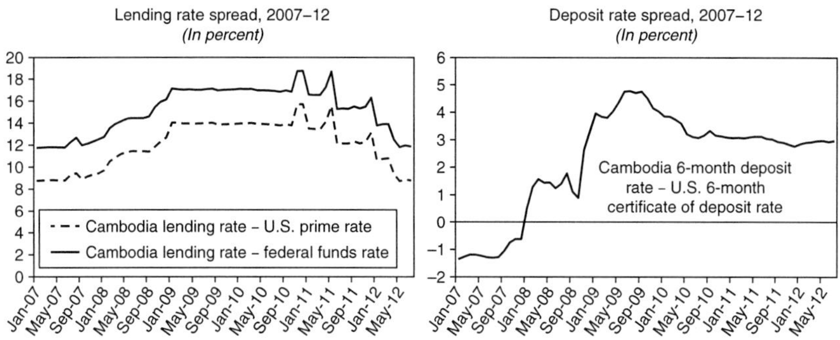

Sources: Data provided by the Cambodian authorities; the Federal Reserve Economic Data; and IMF staff estimates.

mine policy credibility as they create doubt about the enforceability of contracts, thereby inducing residents to hold foreign currency as security. The institutional environment in Cambodia, based on indicators of governance, remains a challenge to private sector and rural development, which are critical economic sectors that use the riel (Figure 3.5). The adoption of an anticorruption law by the Cambodian government in 2010 has been a good step toward improving the institutional environment. However, the country still lags behind other low-income peers in Asia in enforcement of regulations and in rule of law. There is also a need to build the infrastructure—especially electricity, telecommunications, and access to land—in order to support private sector and rural development.

Partly reflecting these structural weaknesses, the interest rate differential between Cambodian and U.S. interest rates has remained high (Figure 3.6). The spread between deposit and lending rates in Cambodia and the United States has been wide, with rates in Cambodia significantly higher. The high interest rate spread reflects several factors, including high country risk, the high cost of banking (including legal uncertainty, litigation costs, and default rates), and low financial intermediation (de Zamaróczy and Sa, 2002). The high interest rate spread is also consistent with findings by Powell and Sturzenegger (2000), who argue that the abolishment of currency risk is offset by an increased default (country) risk premium and that interest rate levels stay significantly higher than in the United States (usually the benchmark).

LESSONS FROM INTERNATIONAL EXPERIENCE

Several countries have successfully dedollarized. Reinhart, Rogoff, and Savastano (2003) separate countries into two categories: (i) those that dedollarized their locally issued foreign currency obligations (examples are Mexico and Argentina); and (ii) those that reduced the share of foreign currency deposits to broad money (examples are Israel, Mexico, Pakistan, and Poland). The latter category is more relevant for Cambodia, given that the country has a high share of foreign currency deposits in broad money and that there are currently no locally issued government securities in foreign currency. In the cases of Israel, Mexico, Pakistan, and Poland, the share of foreign currency deposits in broad money fell by at least 20 percent and settled at a level below that amount.

The following lessons can be drawn from international experiences with dedollarization:

- *Gradual and market-driven policies have been more successful.* Countries in which supportive policies aimed at lowering inflation and deepening financial markets helped reduce dollarization include Chile, Egypt, Israel, and Poland. In these cases, a combination of policies were implemented including: (i) creating markets for local-currency-denominated bonds; (ii) introducing differential remuneration rates on reserve requirements on foreign currency deposits to create a wedge in bank intermediation spreads; and (iii) actively supervising banks to ensure that they fully covered their foreign currency loan positions (Erasmus, Leichter, and Menkulasi, 2009). Further, in the cases of Chile and Israel, indexation was also used successfully to promote local currencies.
- *Forced dedollarization has had macroeconomic costs* (Reinhart, Rogoff, and Savastano, 2003). Forced conversion of dollar deposits into domestic currency was imposed in 1982 and 1998 in Mexico and Pakistan, respectively. Conversion was done using an exchange rate that was substantially lower than the prevailing market rate. While Mexico and Pakistan successfully dedollarized, there were costs. In the case of Mexico, there was substantial capital flight, and private sector bank credit was almost halved in two years; growth suffered significantly and inflation shot up. In the cases of Bolivia and Peru, forced conversion of dollar deposits was subsequently followed by macroeconomic instability that resulted in hyperinflation and led these countries to later allow foreign currency deposits. A similar restriction was introduced in Israel in 1985; however, there it was gradual and market oriented. In Israel's case, a mandatory one-year holding period for all foreign currency deposits was introduced, which made those deposits less attractive than other indexed financial instruments.
- *Reversing dollarization is not easy and is mainly a gradual process.* According to Baliño, Bennett, and Borensztein (1999), dedollarization tends to be difficult, since it depends on institutional changes and occurs when significant benefits can be gained by switching currencies. Dedollarization requires persistence in reducing inflation and stabilizing macroeconomic policy (Erasmus, Leichter, and Menkulasi, 2009). Establishing the credibility of macroeconomic policy is essential.

Cambodia could also draw lessons from the experience of Lao P.D.R. In an attempt to dedollarize, Lao P.D.R. tried to enforce an increased use of the local currency (the kip) by passing a decree (in June 1997) stipulating that only the kip could be used as a medium of exchange in all domestic transactions. This was followed by a depreciation of the kip against the U.S. dollar and the Thai baht (both significant foreign currencies used) as a result of loss of confidence in the kip following the announcement of the measure (Menon, 2008). The share of kip in the money stock fell from about 50 percent to 30 percent, partly due to the valuation effect. Lao P.D.R.'s experience therefore stands as another example of how forced dedollarization could have unintended consequences and thus should be avoided.

POLICY OPTIONS FOR CAMBODIA

In pursuing the goal of promoting greater use of the riel, the Cambodian authorities should consider market-based policies. There is no single silver bullet for encouraging the use of local currency over foreign currency. Rather, a combination of supportive and market-oriented policies is needed. Forced and rapid dedollarization should be avoided, given that it has been unsuccessful elsewhere. Recommended policies for Cambodia are discussed next.

Macroeconomic Environment

A stable macroeconomic environment is critical. Cambodia has achieved macroeconomic stability over the past decade with low inflation, high growth, and a credible fiscal position. The authorities should aim to build upon these achievements. Given the limited tools for conducting monetary policy, continuous buy-in by the fiscal authorities through a prudent fiscal stance is essential. In parallel, it is necessary to establish a credible monetary policy. Since attaining such credibility takes time, the monetary policy authorities should constantly be seen as taking appropriate policy decisions, given economic developments, should be accountable, and should be independent.

A strategy to reduce dollarization should be aligned with an appropriate exchange rate policy. Once dollarization has taken hold, maintaining an independent monetary policy is difficult and therefore exchange rate stabilization becomes a viable option. The NBC has maintained a relatively fixed exchange rate vis-à-vis the U.S. dollar, which has been the effective nominal anchor for three decades in the absence of a formal monetary framework. However, the achievement of low inflation has not halted or reversed the trend of increasing dollarization.[3] Ize and Yeyati (2005) find that dollarization hysteresis (the persistence of dollarization after years of subdued inflation) can be the result of exchange-rate-based stabilization efforts. Monetary policy that closely targets the real exchange rate stimulates dollarization. They further find that if the real exchange rate is stable relative to inflation, the dollar becomes the preferred currency. Therefore, exchange-rate-based stabilization can enforce dollarization and not be well aligned with a dedollarization strategy. Ize and Yeyati (2005) further argue that

[3]Moreover, the relatively fixed exchange rate conflicts with the need to facilitate adjustment to asymmetric shocks as well as to protect official reserves, given the limited lender-of-last resort capability under dollarization.

allowing the exchange rate to be more flexible alters relative risks in favor of the local currency. Kokenyne, Ley, and Veyrune (2010) also find that maintaining trends in the exchange rate could enforce dollarization by entrenching the expectation of a continuous appreciation or depreciation. They argue that a move in the currency in either direction, with less bias toward currency depreciation, helps make foreign exchange risk more apparent and could provide a disincentive to financial dollarization. Given the endogeneity of exchange rate policy, the policy alone is not sufficient for dedollarizing and needs to be put into context with other measures aimed at promoting the use of the local currency.

Domestic Financial Market

The money market needs to be further developed in Cambodia to help reduce risks associated with the dollarization of credit to nontradable sectors and to strengthen the interest rate channel of monetary policy transmission. Developing the money market's ability to forecast and target short-term liquidity is one of the main priorities. There is currently no interbank market in Cambodia; its development should be a priority for the monetary transmission mechanism and for liquidity management.

Several steps are needed to create the interbank market, including establishing the ability of the NBC's Monetary Policy Committee to define a corridor of interest rates for standing facilities. A collateralized rediscount facility could establish a ceiling for the interbank money market, while an overnight deposit facility in the central bank could provide a floor to the interbank rate. Other steps would include developing the NBC's expertise to forecast daily outstanding balances on current accounts of banks that would be used to introduce open market operations; and introducing auctions of NBC certificates to help regulate excess liquidity. How best to sequence the issuance of NBC securities (denominated both in riels and in U.S. dollars) to help develop the interbank market and make further progress in dedollarization is discussed in Part II of this book.

Financial Policy and Prudential Regulation

Several measures could help raise intermediation in the domestic currency and help build a liquidity line of defense.

- First, through the *reserve requirement.* Having a higher reserve requirement on foreign currency liabilities helps make such liabilities more costly. At the same time, this helps mitigate a liquidity risk of dollarization (such as deposit runs) that is related to such deposits. A lower reserve requirement on local currency simultaneously creates an incentive to intermediate in Cambodian riels. The NBC currently maintains a higher reserve requirement on foreign currency than on the riel, helping to promote use of the latter. However, this on its own is not enough to ensure a significant shift toward riel use.
- Second, introducing a *deposit insurance system.* This could foster confidence in the financial system. Insurance coverage should be made higher for the domestic currency than for the foreign currency.

- Third, *maintaining a sufficient level of international reserves.* International reserves play an important role in a dollarized economy as they serve the purpose of liquidity support to banks in case of bank-runs. High coverage of international reserves helps reduce the perception of a weak currency.

Regulation to encourage the use of the riel as a unit of account could help. This could include requiring that all prices in the market be listed in the riel, and that the riel be used for all accounting, financial reporting, and official purposes. The experience of a riel-listing requirement for the newly created stock market shows that such a measure can be effective. Although regulations allow settlement of stock market transactions in U.S. dollars for a transition period of three years, reportedly all transactions have so far been settled in riels, in part reflecting conversion risks. Moreover, the riel is already being used for tax purposes, which is a step in the right direction.

Policies that promote the use of the riel for payments through more convenient and lower-cost services than for foreign currency could be pursued. Peru, for example, introduced a 2 percent tax on checks denominated in foreign currency to discourage the use of foreign currency for payments (Erasmus, Leichter, and Menkulasi, 2009). Also, the riel could be promoted by making it continuously available in larger denominations that are convenient for the public or by introducing a clearance tax for checks denominated in foreign currency.

CONCLUSION

Dollarization in Cambodia has risen in the presence of a stable macroeconomic and political environment. Dollarization appears not to be a problem of currency substitution, given that the volume of riels being used has risen significantly over time. There are several costs associated with dollarization, including a loss of monetary policy and the loss of seigniorage. Also, liquidity and balance sheet risks become heightened. A strategy to reduce dollarization will require making the dollar less attractive compared with the riel. There is no silver bullet, but a comprehensive set of market-driven measures, supported by the continuation of a stable macroeconomic environment, is essential.

APPENDIX

EFFECTS OF CHANGES IN THE U.S. FEDERAL FUNDS RATE ON MACROECONOMIC VARIABLES IN CAMBODIA

The macroeconomic literature identifies two main channels through which monetary policy shocks could be transmitted between countries. The first channel is the *trade channel.* In this channel, monetary policy tightening in a trading partner country (country A) can result in dampened economic activity in that country, leading to lower demand for imports that translates to lower exports in the trading partner country (country B). The second channel is the *financial channel.* When capital is mobile between two countries, the financial channel tends to be important. Monetary policy tightening in country A relative to country B can attract capital to country A given the higher rate of return owing to higher interest rates. The importance of these channels to Cambodia is explored below using a vector autoregression model (VAR).

VECTOR AUTOREGRESSION MODEL

The VAR approach has gained popularity in the economic literature since its introduction by Sims (1980) as a tool to assess the transmission mechanism. In a general form, the VAR(p) model is as follows:

$$y_t = c + \beta_1 y_{t-1} + \beta_2 y_{t-2} + \ldots + \beta_p y_{t-p} + \mu_t$$

where c is an n × 1 vector of constants, β_i is an n × n matrix of betas for i = 1, 2, . . . p and ε_t is an n × 1 vector of error terms. The error terms are serially uncorrelated and the mean of each error vector is the zero vector; the covariance matrix between the error terms for a given point in time is positive definite; and the correlation between the error vectors is zero across time (i.e., there is no serial correlation among the error vectors).

The VAR model is estimated using quarterly data for Cambodia for the period 1995:Q1 to 2009:Q2. The choice of variables in the model is motivated by various theories of the transmission mechanism. While the traditional Mundell-Fleming-Dornbusch model (see Dornbusch, 1980) establishes macroeconomic aspects of transmission in small open economies providing the basis for the trade channel, the model itself has been found in empirical work to be insufficient to explain the full transmission. Therefore, there have been extensions in the literature, including that by Obstfeld and Rogoff (1995), by incorporating the microeconomic aspects of transmission, especially the incorporation of monetary shocks and therefore the important role of interest rates, which help to provide the basis for the financial channel. The variables incorporated in the VAR model are the federal funds rate (for U.S. monetary policy shock); the bilateral nominal exchange rate; the trade balance, which helps to capture the impact on and significance of the trade channel, broad money, domestic lending and deposit interest rates (to help test the significance of the financial channel); inflation; and the output gap (for real economy impact). The output gap is measured as the deviation of real GDP from the historical trend (measured through the Hodrick-Prescott filter). A positive output gap implies that real GDP is above its potential and therefore can have inflationary effects and would warrant domestic tightening.

Tests on Variables and the Model

All variables were found to be integrated of order 1 (I(1)) except the output gap variable, which was found to be integrated of order 0. This means that I(1) variables need to be differenced once to make them stationary. The residuals from the VAR are found to be stationary (Appendix Figure A3.1). The VAR was estimated

Figure A3.1 Residuals

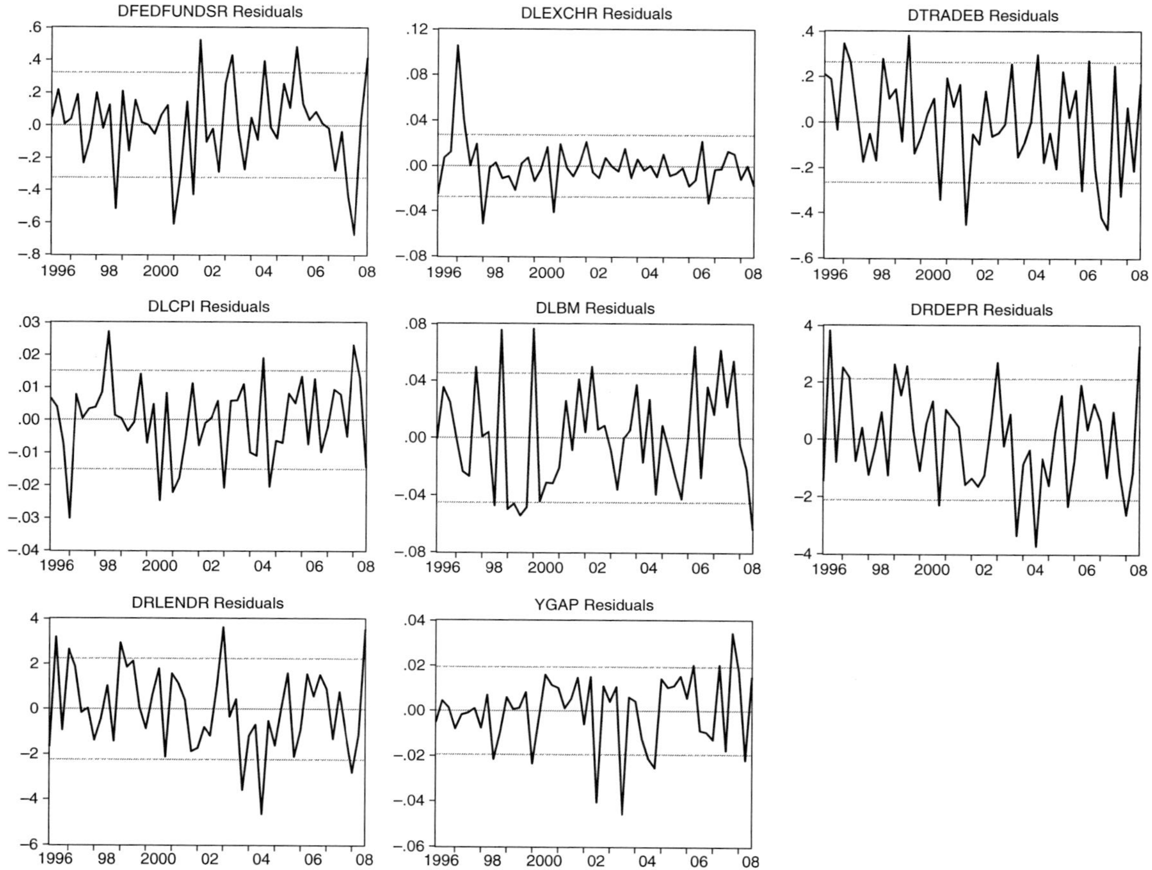

Source: IMF staff estimates.
Note: See text for explanation of abbreviations.

with two lags given that this number of lags minimizes the Akaike information criterion, which helps measure the goodness of fit of the model.

Impulse Response Functions

The responses of variables to the shock in the federal funds rate are identified in the VAR using the Cholesky decomposition (Figure A3.2). The Cholesky method requires identifying the chain of reaction (or the ordering of variables) starting from the exogenous variable to the most endogenous. The ordering used is from the federal funds rate (*DFEDFUNDSR*), to the exchange rate (*DLREXCHR*), to the trade balance (*DTRADEB*), to broad money (*DLBM*), to deposit rates (*DRDEPR*), to lending rates (*DRLENDR*), to the output gap (*YGAP*), and lastly to inflation (*DLCPI*). Oil prices enter exogenously in the model to help capture the effect of commodity prices. In the acronyms of the variables, *d* stands for the differencing and *l* means that the variable has been logged.

It appears that financial sector variables (specifically the lending and deposit rates) have a stronger reaction to shocks in the federal funds rate compared to the trade balance (Figure A3.3). The results can be summarized as follows:

- A one standard deviation shock to the federal funds rate (an increase of about 0.3 percent) results in an increase in the lending rates of about 0.4 percent and a 0.5 percent increase in deposit rates as local banks attempt to minimize the spread between domestic and foreign interest rates. The impact on domestic interest rates occurs within the first quarter of the shock to the federal funds rate, with a larger impact occurring in the second quarter. However, as the lag of the impact increases, domestic interest rates decline (between five and seven months following the shock) probably reacting at this point to lower demand for loans as the Cambodian economy contracts.
- A shock to the federal funds rate appears to result in an increase in the Cambodian trade balance (by about 0.1 percent following a 0.3 percent shock in the federal funds rate) within a quarter and a negative effect in two quarters. The immediate positive impact may reflect a stronger contractionary impact on imports in Cambodia, since as domestic interest rates also respond with an increase, they contribute to an overall contraction. However, the trade balance worsens in the third quarter, indicating the contractionary effect on exports as U.S. demand has had time to respond to the initial federal funds rate shock.
- The response of the exchange rate is small, with the riel depreciating against the U.S. dollar. This is not surprising owing to the high dollarization in Cambodia, which implies a loss of flexibility in exchange rate policy. Some economists have contended that highly dollarized economies tend to adjust through goods and factor markets, as well as financial markets, and not necessarily through the exchange rate (de Zamaróczy and Sa, 2003).
- A shock to the federal funds rate results in a decline in output and inflation in Cambodia, reflecting a contractionary effect of U.S. monetary policy

Figure A3.2 Impulse Responses

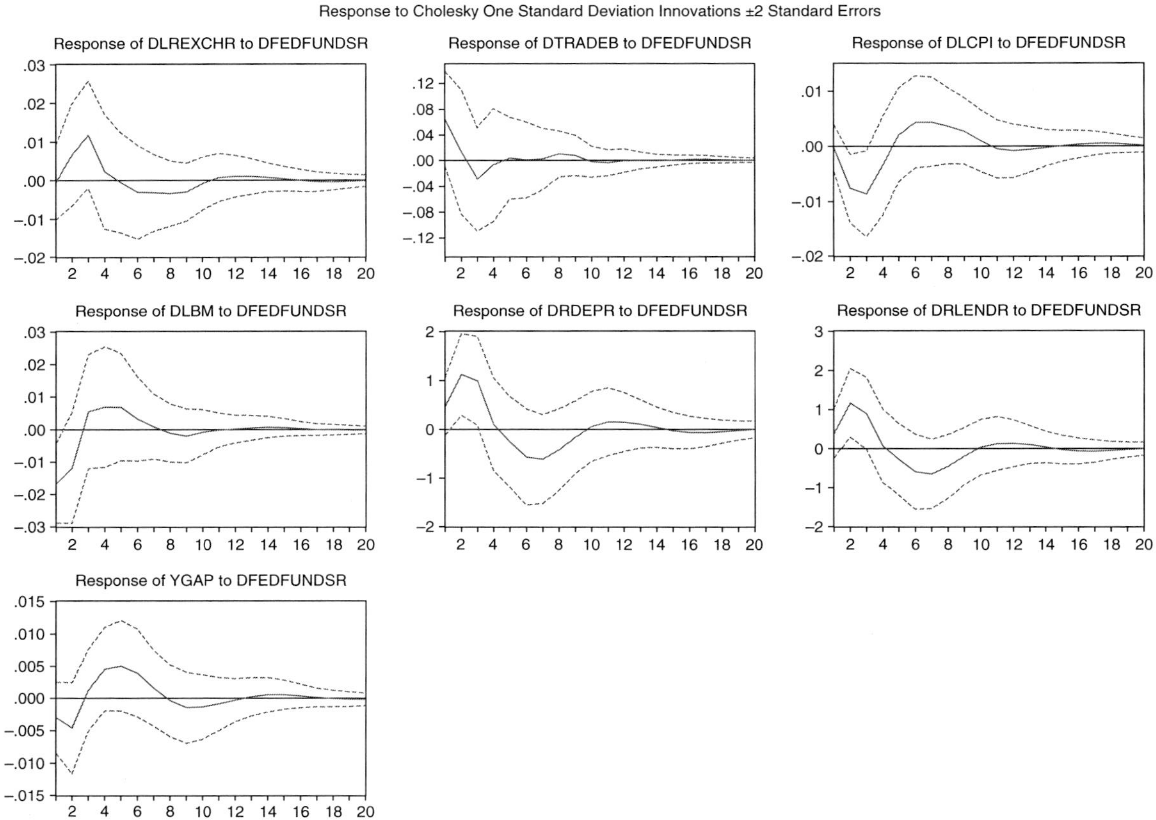

Source: IMF staff estimates.
Note: The dotted lines are response standard errors. See text for explanation of abbreviations.

Figure A3.3 Cumulative Pass-Through Coefficients of the Federal Funds Rate

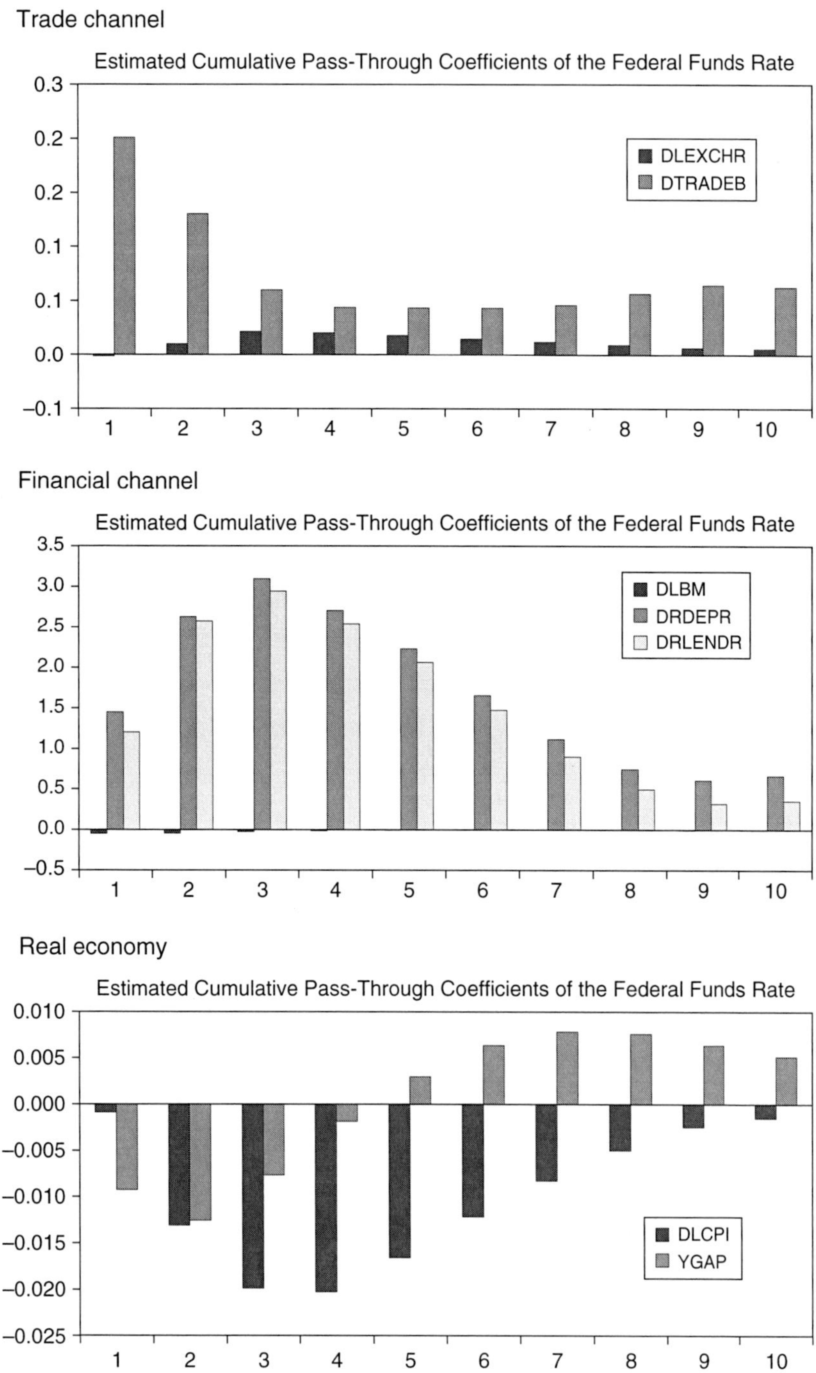

Source: IMF staff estimates.
Note: See text for explanation of abbreviations.

Figure A3.4 Variance Decompositions

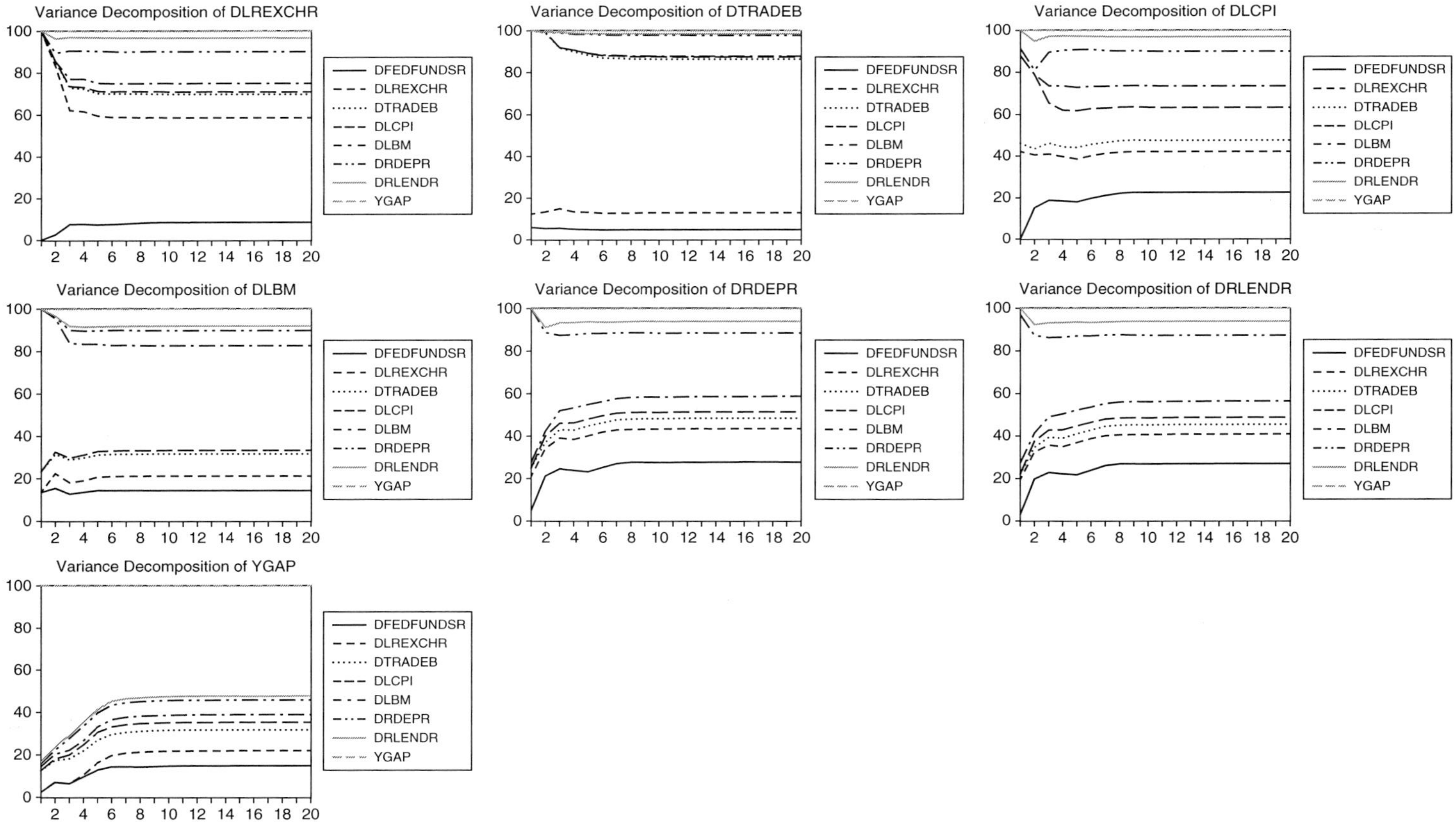

Source: IMF staff estimates.
Note: See text for explanation of abbreviations.

(and therefore lower liquidity into Cambodia) as well as the contractionary effect of domestic interest rates within the first quarter. However, as domestic interest rates decline in the following months, domestic output picks up and inflation rises a quarter later.

Variance Decompositions

Another way to analyze the dynamics of the VAR is through forecast error variance decompositions. The variance decompositions help to determine the relative importance of the shock variable to fluctuations in the response variables in the model (Figure A3.4). Shocks to the federal funds rate contribute about 25 percent of variation in the financial variables, whereas they contribute about 5 percent of the variation in the trade balance. On real economy variables, the federal funds rate contributes to about 15 percent of variation in the output gap and about 23 percent of variation in Cambodian inflation. The higher impact on the real economy compared to the trade channel likely reflects the double impact of the financial and the trade channels on overall economic activity.

REFERENCES

Baliño, T., A. Bennett, and E. Borensztein, 1999, "Monetary Policy in Dollarized Economies," IMF Occasional Paper No. 171 (Washington: International Monetary Fund).

Berg, A., and E. Borensztein, 2000, "Full Dollarization: The Pros and Cons," *IMF Economic Issues,* No. 24 (Washington: International Monetary Fund).

Bogetić, Ž., 2000, "The Calculus of Full Dollarization," *Central Banking,* Vol. 11 (November), pp. 45–57.

Chang, R., 2000, "Dollarization: A Scorecard," *Economic Review* (Federal Reserve Bank of Atlanta), Vol. 85, No. 3, pages 1–11.

Coe, D. T., I. Lee, W. F. Abdelati, D. Eastman, R. P. Hagemann, S. Ishikawa, A. Lopez-Mejia, S. Mitra, K. Nakamura, N. Rendak, S. Yelten, and S. Muñoz, 2006, *Cambodia: Rebuilding for a Challenging Future* (Washington: International Monetary Fund).

de Zamaróczy, M., and S. Sa, 2002, "Macroeconomic Adjustment in a Highly Dollarized Economy: The Case of Cambodia," IMF Working Paper No. 02/92 (Washington: International Monetary Fund).

———, 2003, "Economic Policy in a Highly Dollarized Economy: The Case of Cambodia," IMF Occasional Paper No. 219 (Washington: International Monetary Fund).

Dornbusch, R., 1980, *Open Economy Macroeconomics* (New York: Basic Books).

Duma, N., 2011, "Dollarization in Cambodia: Causes and Policy Implications," IMF Working Paper No. 49 (Washington: International Monetary Fund).

Erasmus, L., J. Leichter, and J. Menkulasi, 2009, "Dedollarization in Liberia—Lessons from Cross-Country Experience," IMF Working Paper 09/37 (Washington: International Monetary Fund).

Galindo, A., and L. Leiderman, 2005, "Living with Dollarization and the Route to Dedollarization," Working Paper No. 526 (Washington: Inter-American Development Bank).

Goux, J., and C. Cordahi, 2007, "The International Transmission of Monetary Shocks in a Dollarized Economy: The Case of USA and Lebanon," GATE Working Paper No. 07–15, Groupe d'Analyse et de Théorie Économique, France.

Herrera, L., and R. Valdés, 2005, "Dedollarization, Indexation and Nominalization: The Chilean Experience," *The Journal of Policy Reform,* Vol. 8, No. 4, pp. 281–312.

Humpage, O., 2002, "An Incentive-Compatible Suggestion for Seigniorage Sharing with Dollarizing Countries," Policy Discussion Paper No. 4 (Cleveland: Federal Reserve Bank of Cleveland).

Ize, A., and E. Yeyati, 2005, "Financial De-Dollarization: Is It for Real?" IMF Working Paper No. 05/187 (Washington: International Monetary Fund).

Kim, S., 2001, "International Transmission of US Monetary Policy Shocks: Evidence from VAR's," *Journal of Monetary Economics,* Vol. 48, pp. 339–72.

Kokenyne, A., J. Ley, and R. Veyrune, 2010, "Dedollarization," IMF Working Paper No. 10/188 (Washington: International Monetary Fund).

Menon, J., 2008, "Cambodia's Persistent Dollarization: Causes and Policy Options," Working Paper on Regional Economic Integration No. 19 (Manila: Asian Development Bank)

Obstfeld, M., and K. Rogoff, 1995, "The Mirage of Fixed Exchange Rates," NBER Working Paper No. 5191 (Cambridge, MA: National Bureau of Economic Research).

Powell, A., and F. Sturzenegger, 2000, "Dollarization: The Link between Devaluation and Default Risk," Business School, Universidad Torcuato Di Tella, Buenos Aires.

Prasso, S., 2001, "The Riel Value of Money: How the World's Only Attempt to Abolish Money Has Hindered Cambodia's Economic Development," *Asia Pacific Issues,* No. 49 (Honolulu: East-West Center).

Reinhart, C., K. Rogoff, and M. Savastano, 2003, "Addicted to Dollars," NBER Working Paper No. 10015 (Cambridge, MA: National Bureau of Economic Research).

Rennhack, R., and M. Nozaki, 2006, "Financial Dollarization in Latin America," IMF Working Paper No. 06/7 (Washington: International Monetary Fund).

Sims, C. A., 1980, "Macroeconomics and Reality," *Econometrica,* Vol. 48, No. 1 (January), pp. 1–48.

Unteroberdoerster, O., 2002, "Foreign Currency Deposits in Vietnam—Trends and Policy Issues," in *Vietnam: Selected Issues and Statistical Appendix,* IMF Country Report No. 02/5 (Washington: International Monetary Fund).

CHAPTER 4

Cambodia's Banking Sector: Are More Banks Always Better?

FAISAL AHMED AND PHURICHAI RUNGCHAROENKITKUL

Cambodia has witnessed a rapid increase in the number of banks in recent years. This chapter explores whether Cambodia is "overbanked" from a cross-country perspective.[1] It also discusses how such a proliferation of banks could adversely affect competition and financial stability given the ownership structure and fragmentation in the banking system, highlighting the need for putting a moratorium on new bank licenses and further improving supervision.

Cambodia is overbanked compared with its developmental peers and neighbors, including even countries with significantly higher income levels and much larger and better developed financial systems. An overbanked financial system implies a less than optimal balance between competitiveness and soundness in the banking system; indeed, a proliferation of banks can weaken financial stability including by encouraging banks in excessive risk taking, limiting the scope for business diversification, and overburdening the banking system's supervisory capacity (Claessens and Laeven, 2004). Unlike other industries, in a banking system competition is related less to the number of institutions and more to the quality of supervision and transparency. Furthermore, excessive competition to capture an already saturated market can pose risks to the health of the banking system.

The risks to financial stability in Cambodia could increase owing to a confluence of Cambodia-specific structural factors: (i) a high level of dollarization (Chapter 3), limiting the role of the central bank as a lender of last resort; (ii) the absence of an interbank market, constraining risk sharing and liquidity management; (iii) limited fiscal buffers and foreign exchange reserves to support the banking system in times of stress; (iv) regulatory and supervisory constraints from overbanking; and (v) still fragile confidence in the banking system given Cambodia's history of civil war.

Although foreign-owned entrants to the banking system can serve as conduits for international best practices and newer sources of funding, financial stability risks could easily emerge, because excessive bank flows can amplify macroeconomic

[1]The notion of "overbanking" does not refer to financial penetration, that is, financial access, which is currently low in Cambodia at 10 percent of the population. Rather, it refers to the density of banks (i.e., the number of banks for a given level of credit, economic activity, or population, as used in the literature; see Claessens and Laeven, 2004).

and financial sector vulnerabilities. The latter problem was witnessed in emerging Europe during the most recent financial crisis and, in earlier decades, in East Asia and Latin America. The shifting funding structure of the banking system—an increasing reliance on external sources—warrants closer monitoring. It also highlights the need for exploring options for managing externally funded credit growth to complement the reserve requirement.

STYLIZED FEATURES OF THE CAMBODIAN BANKING SYSTEM

Reversing the consolidation of and subsequent stability in the number of banks until about 2005, since then Cambodia's banking system has become increasingly crowded, with the number of banks more than doubling to 39 (Figure 4.1). Many of the new entrants are foreign banks with operations that, although clustered in select urban centers such as Phnom Penh, intermediate a sizable amount of loans.

Cambodia's banking system is both highly liberalized and highly dollarized,[2] and foreign banks have a relatively large presence in it as compared with other countries in the region. More than two-thirds of the banks, which account for half the total deposits, are foreign-owned (Figure 4.2). Most of the foreign banks

Figure 4.1 Cambodia: Rapidly Increasing Number of Banks

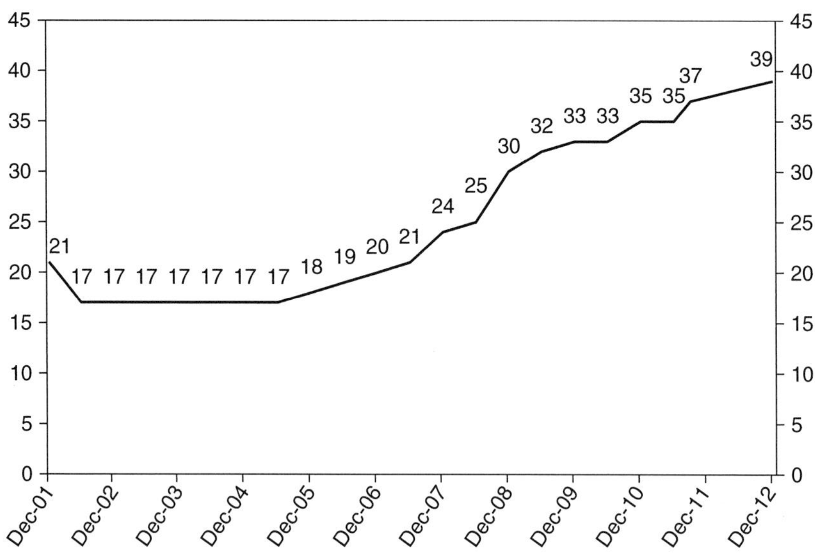

Source: National Bank of Cambodia.

[2]As of December 2012, over 95 percent of deposits and lending was in U.S. dollars.

originate in neighboring countries and display significant variation in size and scope of operations (Figure 4.3).[3]

The banking system is relatively concentrated but populated by a large cluster of small banks, with 25 (out of 39) banks accounting for less than 10

Figure 4.2 Ownership Structure of Banks in Cambodia: Domestic versus Foreign

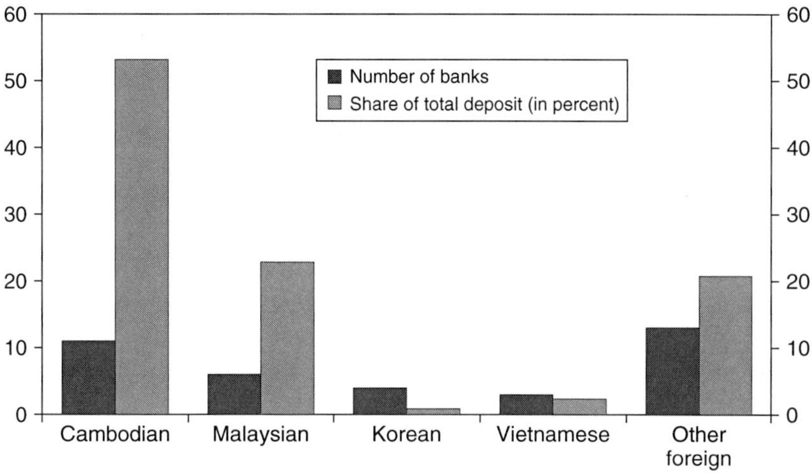

Source: National Bank of Cambodia.

Note: Defined as the residency of majority ownership. "Other foreign" includes banks from Australia (ANZ Royal), China, India, Japan, Kazakhstan, Taiwan Province of China, Thailand, and the United States.

Figure 4.3 Cambodia: Banking System Structure—Size Distribution of Banks, December 2011

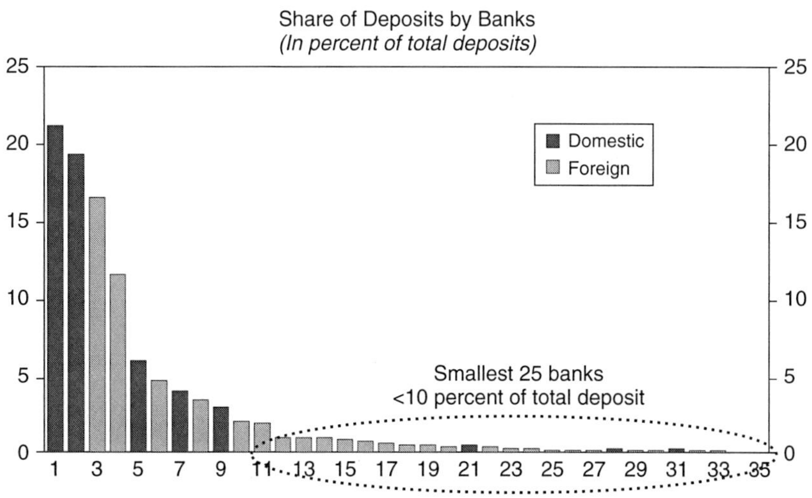

Source: National Bank of Cambodia.

[3]Five of the top 10 largest banks are foreign-owned (Figure 4.3).

percent of total deposits.[4] Some of the smaller banks have attempted to rapidly increase their portfolios in recent years, albeit from a small base. Some of the recent entrants have captured a sizable market share within a short period. Although some of the larger banks have their preferred market segments, overall competition for market share has increased sharply in the last two years as demonstrated by the substantial decline in interest rate spreads over the same period.

A CONCENTRATED BANKING SYSTEM

The banking system in Cambodia is characterized by "a missing middle"—that is, there are a few large banks and a large number of small banks. Although this concentration has eased somewhat, when compared to Vietnam, a neighbor with a higher per capita income and larger financial system, the concentration appears to be more acute in Cambodia. The large banks individually are also more dominant in Cambodia (Figure 4.4).

The traditional indicators of concentration (e.g., a Herfindahl index of the share of bank deposits or credit in the top banks) also point to a relatively concentrated banking sector in Cambodia, further highlighting the need for improving supervision and corporate governance to increase contestability and efficiency in the banking system (Figure 4.4).

Figure 4.4 Comparing Bank Concentration: Cambodia and Vietnam *(Distribution in percent of total deposits from largest to smallest banks, 2010 or latest)*

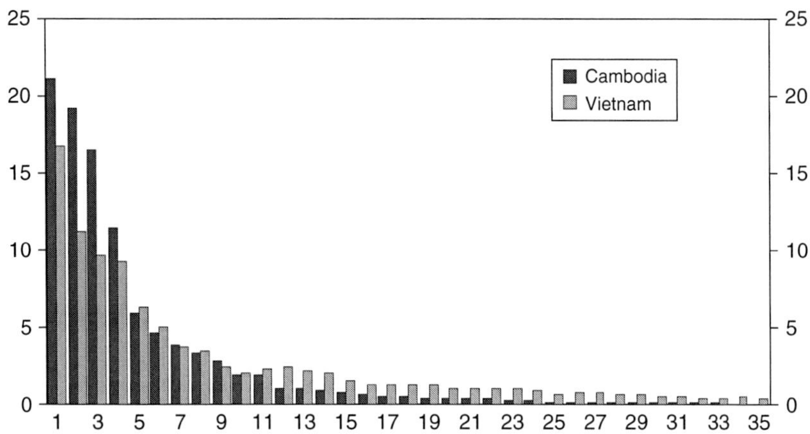

Sources: Bankscope; the National Bank of Cambodia, and IMF staff estimates.

[4]A few of the specialized banks are restricted from taking domestic deposits.

IS CAMBODIA "OVERBANKED"?

To answer this question, we use four indicators of bank density: (i) number of banks per unit of credit; (ii) number of banks per unit of output; (iii) number of banks for a given size of population; and (iv) number of banks for a given number of the "banked" population (defined as population adjusted for financial penetration). We then compare bank density across Cambodia's developmental peers and neighbors.

By all four indicators, Cambodia appears overbanked, standing out as an outlier compared with developmental peers and neighboring countries (Figure 4.5). Even compared with Vietnam, which has the second highest number of banks in the region (91, second to Indonesia with 121 banks) and is facing elevated financial stability risks, the number of banks in Cambodia, measured per unit of credit, is 10 times higher, and measured relative to GDP (output) it is three times higher.

The degree of overbanking in Cambodia, therefore, appears to be pronounced, especially in light of the country's low level of financial access (see World Bank,

Figure 4.5 How "Overbanked" Is Cambodia? *(Indicators of bank "density")*

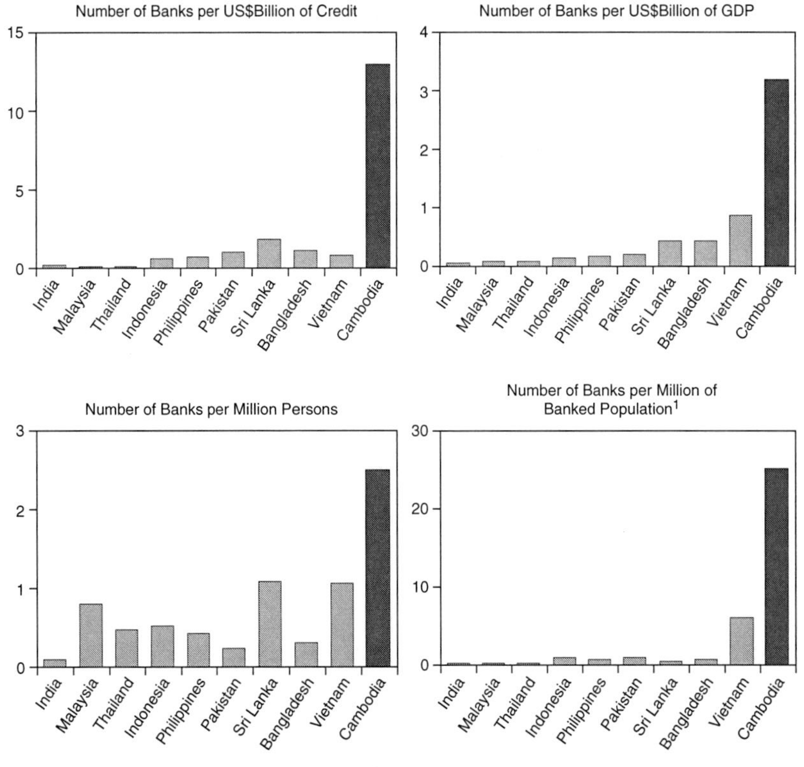

Sources: Central banks; Moody's; CGAP and World Bank Group, Financial Access Database 2010; and IMF staff estimates.
[1]"Banked population" is calculated as population adjusted for financial penetration ratio.

2010 and Figure 4.5). It should be noted that, in terms of providing financial access to a large segment of the population, microfinance institutions are playing a key role and some of the commercial banks are considering increasing their presence in this business segment.

HOW OVERBANKING AFFECTS FINANCIAL STABILITY

Given the banking structure in Cambodia—a few large banks along with a large cluster of small banks—one question naturally arises: What are the likely effects of the proliferation of banks on competition and financial stability (see also Box 4.1)?[5]

An overcrowded banking sector implies reduced market power and profit and thus a lower buffer against adverse shocks for a given level and quality of bank capitalization (Allen and Gale, 2004). A reduced scope for profit also incentivizes small banks to pursue more aggressive risk-taking behavior, increasing overall systemic risk (Vives, 2001). Any excessive competition to capture market share in a small and saturated market can pose further risks to banks' long-term profitability and soundness.

In Cambodia, many of the small banks operate in niche markets, limiting the scope for diversification in their portfolios.[6] In addition, small banks often do not have the requisite size to benefit from economies of scale (e.g., internal risk management and credit quality control) (Beck, Demirgüç-Kunt, and Levine, 2006). This again tends to lower profits and increase incentives for risk taking.

BOX 4.1

Nexus Between Competition and Financial Stability

The relationship between competition and financial stability is complex; competition does not necessarily lead to financial stability, and excessive competition can lead to financial fragility, supporting the notion of an optimal level of competition for a given level of financial development and structure.

Vives (2001) argues that different countries may have different optimal levels of competition intensity; countries with a strong regulatory structure and relatively low social costs of failure (e.g., few government bailouts, low unemployment) will benefit from intense rivalry. On the other hand, developing countries with a weak institutional structure and high social costs of failure should moderate the intensity of competition and focus on improving regulation and supervision. Although in advanced economies competition can foster financial stability, Berger, Klapper, and Turk-Ariss (2009) find that excessive competition in developing countries weakens financial stability, in line with the competition-fragility nexus argued in Allen and Gale (2004).

---

[5]Claessens and Laeven (2004) refer to evidence in the industrial organization literature, which underscores that measures of market structure, such as the number of institutions, are not necessarily related to the level of competitiveness in an industry.

[6]It should be noted that large banks in developing countries also are not immune to concentration risks and connected lending due to challenges with corporate governance and bank supervision. As seen during the recent global financial crisis, banks in advanced economies are also exposed to a large set of risks, including high leverage.

The presence of a large number of small banks can complicate the already weak monetary transmission channel in Cambodia, as is common in many developing countries. Since small banks have been observed to be more vulnerable to liquidity shocks, the conduct of monetary policy or imposition of stronger capital adequacy standards can become more challenging, as has been witnessed in Vietnam (see Box 4.2).

Overbanking, coupled with the ownership structure, can amplify the buildup of financial stability risks. For example, domestic liquidity and bank flows through foreign banks at low interest rates can accelerate the race to capture market share and result in the lowering of credit standards. In fact, cheaper foreign funding and ample domestic liquidity in Cambodia have resulted in a significant decline in lending interest rates; the interest rate spread was compressed by around 150–200 basis points over the 12 months up to December 2012, raising questions about the adequate pricing of risks and the downward pressure on bank profitability as measured by the return on assets.[7]

BOX 4.2

Vietnam's Experience with Small Banks

Amid an optimistic investor assessment following its integration into the World Trade Organization, Vietnam received a large number of applications from new banks. During 2007–08, nine new banks were given licenses and another nine banks were authorized to change from a limited rural scope to unrestricted urban operations, leading to a significant increase in the number of banks and increasing competition for deposits and scarce human resources.

Many of the new (and small) banks started to compete aggressively for funding (deposits and/or interbank credit) and participated in connected lending, contributing to the buildup of the credit boom and exacerbating Vietnam's current financial sector vulnerabilities. Many of the small banks were undercapitalized, poorly managed, and exposed to excessive risks. Reportedly, during 2007 and afterward, in these banks credit growth was extremely fast, the funding costs to this growth were high, and exposures to the stock market and real estate bubbles were elevated. Furthermore, the governance structure of many of these small banks weakened their credit allocation process and thus their credit quality. Some of these banks aggressively expanded their portfolios, often into illiquid assets such as real estate.

The financial stability risks and liquidity concerns of the small banks complicated the implementation of regulatory and supervisory measures (e.g., resulting in repeated delays in enforcing the minimum capital requirements). Furthermore, the liquidity risks of the small banks complicated monetary policy. The loose monetary conditions also accelerated the buildup of macro-financial vulnerability. The banking system in Vietnam is now undergoing consolidation.

---

[7]Although most of the traditional financial soundness indicators, such as nonperforming loans or sectoral loan classification data, do not point toward any immediate vulnerabilities, it should be noted that those indicators are often backward looking and may not adequately capture the medium-term risks at the early stage of the credit cycle.

Compounding the above financial stability risks is the fact that a crowded banking system is more difficult to monitor, in turn burdening the generally constrained supervisory capacity common in developing countries (diseconomies of scale in supervision). In Cambodia, this capacity, while improving in recent years, may be stretched because of the growing number of banks (see Chapter 9 for a detailed discussion).

All of the channels discussed above appear to be relevant for Cambodia and warrant continued vigilance by supervisors. Moreover, given that most of the small banks operate in urban centers (mostly in Phnom Penh) and offer a narrow set of products and services, the scope for diversification remains limited. The banks' small size puts an additional constraint on their ability to optimize risk management practices that benefit from economies of scale.

HOW FOREIGN OWNERSHIP AFFECTS MACRO-FINANCIAL STABILITY

Although foreign banks can contribute positively to the efficiency of the banking system, including through the implementation of international best practices, better risk management, and product innovation, they are not risk-free and do not necessarily offset the consequent financial-stability risks from overbanking. In fact, cheaper funding through foreign banks can easily trigger a credit boom and lower credit standards in a small domestic market. These risks are important given the large degree of foreign ownership in the Cambodian banking system.

Empirical studies of foreign bank behavior show that large foreign ownership increases the likelihood of importing the home countries' macroeconomic and policy volatilities (Clark and others, 2003). Bank flows are generally short term, procyclical, and more volatile in times of crisis. Since many of the foreign-owned banks in Cambodia are from parts of Asia that have attracted global capital flows (reflecting improved regional growth prospects), Cambodian policymakers need to be mindful of the consequences of capital inflows through the banking system.

Indications are that some of the banks in Cambodia have already started sourcing cheaper funds from abroad to finance domestic lending. Net foreign assets fell steadily during 2012, driven by rising foreign liabilities (Figure 4.6). The diverging pattern in 2012 of net foreign assets and net domestic assets was similar to the pattern observed during the 2007–08 credit boom, indicating a rising risk appetite in the domestic credit market.

Structurally, since 2011 credit growth has been outpacing deposit growth, and it is now being aided by a marked increase in cross-border bank flows (both non-resident deposits and other foreign liabilities), which tend to be more volatile than other forms of capital flow. Bank-level diagnostics show credit growth in Cambodia has been higher in smaller banks and has accelerated with the entry of foreign banks, which accounted for more than two-thirds of the 2012 credit flows, increasing the sensitivity of the banking system to external funding shocks. These risks are now structurally pronounced given that credit growth in Cambodia is clearly breaking away from its long-term pace of financial deepening (see Chapter 5).

Figure 4.6 Cambodia: Net Foreign and Domestic Assets in Deposit Money Banks *(In percent of GDP)*

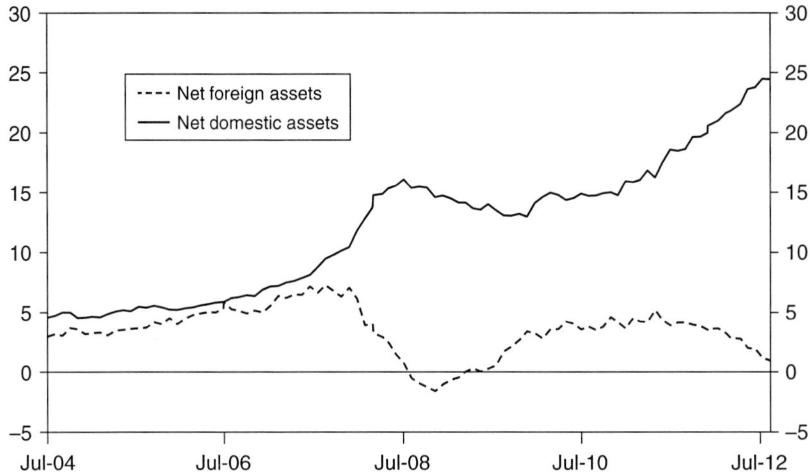

Source: National Bank of Cambodia; and IMF staff estimates.

Studies on emerging Europe (which shares the Cambodian feature of large foreign ownership of the banking system and reliance on external funding) suggest that foreign bank behavior can be procyclical, aggravating macroeconomic and financial stability risks (Box 4.3). De Haas and Van Horen (2011) showed that foreign bank subsidiaries in emerging Europe reduced their lending earlier and faster than domestic banks during the 2008–09 global financial crisis.[8]

In Cambodia, the influx of mostly foreign banks highlights the importance of ratcheting up bank supervision as well as the critical need for better coordination,

BOX 4.3

Possible Banking Lessons for Cambodia from Emerging Europe

The expansion of Western European banks to emerging Europe fueled a credit boom before the global financial crisis. These banks provided direct cross-border lending and financed much of the credit increase in emerging Europe through interbank deposits and capital injections to their local subsidiaries. With low interest margins in Western Europe, they became increasingly interested in expanding in emerging Europe and came to dominate much of the latter region's banking systems.

Capital inflows through these banks fueled a domestic credit boom in emerging Europe, which led not only to rapid GDP growth but also to sharply wider current account deficits and overheating pressures. Capital inflows increasingly went to the

[8]Japanese banks during the Asian crisis and North American banks during the Argentine crisis also sharply reduced their lending.

nontradable sectors (financial services, real estate, and construction) and growth became unbalanced and vulnerable to a sudden reversal of capital flows. Moreover, since the majority of loans were foreign-currency-denominated in much of the region, an exchange rate depreciation resulting from a slowdown of capital flows would have had powerful adverse balance sheet effects and could have undermined financial stability. Because much of the external debt was owed by banks, financial stability was potentially also at risk from this perspective.

In the fall of 2008, the large capital flows from banks in advanced economies to emerging Europe declined suddenly. In the global financial turmoil, global risk aversion increased sharply, stock markets fell precipitously, and interbank markets dried up. Banks in advanced economies, which were confronted with liquidity and capital shortages, came under severe liquidity pressures, which forced them to stop new lending or even to deleverage. In a change of strategy, they advised their subsidiaries that new funding would henceforth need to come from increasing local deposits. Other capital inflows to the region declined as well, further exacerbating the economic downturn.

The regulatory response to the banks' problems in the home markets in Western Europe risked aggravating the reversal of credit flows. Starting in the fall of 2008, parent banks faced mounting liquidity and solvency problems in their domestic markets, and most of the banks needed to avail themselves of some form of state aid in their home countries. In a number of cases, home regulators pressed for deleveraging from investments in Eastern Europe. In the end, although some of the Western banks played a stabilizing role, banking systems in several emerging European countries could not avoid crises (e.g., the Baltic countries, Hungary, and Ukraine).

The experience of emerging Europe highlights how bank flows, including even those that pass through the prudently managed foreign banks, can contribute to a rapid buildup of financial stability risk and create policy challenges as external financial conditions change. The existing tools for managing credit growth (i.e., reserve requirements on deposits) cannot directly alter the pace of foreign-funded intermediation. Given Cambodia's open capital account and dollarization, the pace of risk buildup therefore needs to be closely managed and supervised.

Sources: International Monetary Fund, 2010; and Purfield and Rosenberg, 2010.

cooperation, and information exchange among cross-border supervisors to anticipate and minimize financial stability risks. To improve bank supervision, therefore, it is important to prevent the banking system from overcrowding, including by instituting a moratorium on new bank licenses.[9]

CONCLUSION

Cambodia appears to be "overbanked" when compared with its developmental peers and neighboring countries. An overbanked financial system does not necessarily imply an optimal balance between competitiveness and soundness in

[9]Entrants are reported to be attracted to the Cambodian market because of its growth potential. Some of the foreign banks from neighboring countries (e.g., Vietnam) are reportedly influenced by both pull factors (e.g., growth potential in the host market) and push factors (saturated home market).

the banking system. In fact, it can accelerate risk buildup, including through excessive risk-taking behavior by the banks, limiting the scope for diversification and overburdening supervisory capacity. Given Cambodia's open capital account, high level of dollarization, and limited monetary policy tools, the financial stability risks from a crowded banking system need to be closely monitored and supervised, especially when credit growth results from increasingly volatile foreign bank flows.

REFERENCES

Allen, Franklin, and Douglas Gale, 2004, "Competition and Financial Stability," *Journal of Money, Credit, and Banking,* Vol. 36, No. 3, Part 2, pp. 453–80.

Beck, Thorsten, Asli Demirgüç-Kunt, and Ross Levine, 2006, "Bank Concentration, Competition, and Crises: First Results," *Journal of Banking and Finance,* Vol. 30, pp. 1581–1603.

Berger, Allen, Leora Klapper, and Rima Turk-Ariss, 2009, "Bank Competition and Financial Stability," *Journal of Financial Services Research,* Vol. 35, No. 2, pp. 99–118.

Bikker, Jacob A., and Katharina Haaf, 2002, "Competition, Concentration and Their Relationship: An Empirical Analysis of the Banking Industry," *Journal of Banking and Finance,* Vol. 26, pp. 2191–214.

Cerutti, Eugenio, Anna Ilyina, Yulia Makarova, and Christian Schmeider, 2010, "Bankers Without Borders? Implications of Ring-Fencing for European Cross-Border Banks," IMF Working Paper No. 10/247 (Washington: International Monetary Fund)

Claessens, Stijn, and Luc Laeven, 2004, "What Drives Bank Competition? Some International Evidence," *Journal of Money, Credit and Banking,* Vol. 36, No. 3, pp. 563–83.

Clark, George, Robert Cull, Maria Soledad Martinez Peria, and Susana Sanchez, 2003, "Foreign Bank Entry: Experience, Implications for Developing Economies, and Agenda for Further Research," *The World Bank Research Observer,* Vol. 18, No. 1 (Spring), pp. 25–59 (Oxford University Press).

Consultative Group to Assist the Poor (CGAP) and World Bank Group, "Financial Access 2010," Database. Available via the Internet at http://www.cgap.org/data/financial-access-2010-database-cgap.

De Haas, Ralph, Yevgeniya Korniyenko, Elena Loukoianova, and Alexander Pivovarsky, 2012, "Foreign Banks and the Vienna Initiative: Turning Sinners into Saints?" IMF Working Paper No. 12/117 (Washington, International Monetary Fund).

De Haas, Ralph, and Neeltje Van Horen, 2011, "Running for the Exit: International Banks and Crisis Transmission," Working Paper No. 124 (London: European Bank for Reconstruction and Development).

De Haas, Ralph, and Iman Van Lelyveld, 2006, "Foreign Banks and Credit Stability in Central and Eastern Europe: A Panel Data Analysis," *Journal of Banking and Finance,* Vol. 30, pp. 1927–52.

De Nicolò, G., and Elena Loukoianova, 2007, "Bank Ownership, Market Structure and Risk," IMF Working Paper No. 07/215 (Washington: International Monetary Fund).

International Monetary Fund, 2010, *Regional Economic Outlook: Europe* (Washington, October).

Purfield, Catriona, and Christoph B. Rosenberg, 2010, "Adjustment Under a Currency Peg: Estonia, Latvia, and Lithuania during the Global Financial Crisis 2008–09," IMF Working Paper No. 10/213 (Washington: International Monetary Fund).

Schaeck, Klaus, Martin Čihák, and Simon Wolfe, 2006, "Are More Competitive Banking Systems More Stable?" IMF Working Paper No. 06/143 (Washington: International Monetary Fund).

Vives, Xavier, 2001, "Competition in the Changing World of Banking," *Oxford Review of Economic Policy,* Vol. 17, No. 4, pp. 535–47.

World Bank, 2010, *Financial Access: The State of Financial Inclusion Through the Crisis* (Washington).

CHAPTER 5

What Can Go Wrong? Shifting Vulnerabilities as Asia Rebalances

FAISAL AHMED, JUNG YEON KIM, AND NUJIN SUPHAPHIPHAT

At the current juncture, Cambodia is displaying some hybrid economic features—still mostly those of a low-income country but including some aspects of an emerging market economy. It best exemplifies this duality in the concentrated production structure of a low-income country and the capital account openness of an emerging market economy. This chapter provides an overview of Cambodia's economic vulnerabilities, given its ongoing economic transformation and taking into consideration the country's unique features and economic structure. We show that external shocks can explain more than half of Cambodia's growth variation, a trend that is expected to accelerate in the years ahead as its integration with the global economy, and with emerging Asia in particular, expands and deepens. In this context, we explore the likely evolution of vulnerabilities by sector—external, financial, and fiscal—and their interactions over time. We conclude by advocating a virtuous cycle of vulnerability-mitigating policies to make growth more resilient.

CAMBODIA: VULNERABILITY ANALYSIS IN THE CONTEXT OF LOW-INCOME COUNTRIES

Before delving into Cambodia-specific discussion, some stylized facts about low-income countries and their vulnerabilities are in order.

When compared to middle- and high-income countries, low-income countries tend to have greater output, consumption, and investment volatility (Table 5.1), reflecting an interplay of structural and external shocks.[1]

Recent empirical work finds that low-income countries and, in some cases, emerging market economies face a higher probability of financial sector (e.g., banking and currency) and terms of trade shocks (Table 5.2). In low-income countries in the past decade external shocks have also been of growing importance as a source of macroeconomic volatility (IMF, 2010, 2011a).

[1]Macroeconomic volatility and growth tend to be negatively correlated through various types of uncertainty (e.g., economic, political, and policy-related) and through binding constraints on investment, such as low saving and limited financial development (Loayza and others, 2007).

TABLE 5.1

Output, Consumption, and Investment Volatility, 1970–2004 *(median)*

	Low-income	Middle-income	High-income
σ[y]*	0.062	0.0627	0.0312
σ[c]/σ[y]	1.16	1.11	1.02
σ[i]/σ[y]	3.69	3.51	3.41

Source: Tabova (2009).
*σ[y], σ[c], and σ[i] represent standard deviation of agregate output, consumption, and investment, respectively.

TABLE 5.2

Frequency of Shocks Across Country Groups 1970–2007

	Frequency of Shocks					
	Low-income countries		Emerging markets		Advanced economies	
	Total number	Probability (In percent of country years)	Total number	Probability (In percent of country years)	Total number	Probability (In percent of country years)
Financial and Macro-economic Shocks						
Banking crisis	51	1.9	53	3.2	13	1.1
Currency crisis	99	3.8	69	4.1	13	1.1
Debt crisis	28	1.1	28	1.7	0	0
Reversal of capital flows	405	15.4	141	8.5	46	3.9
Country-specific external shocks						
Terms of trade shock	453	17.2	160	9.6	45	3.8
Natural disaster	72	2.8	35	2.1	17	1.4

Source: IMF (2011a).

In Cambodia, as in many other low-income countries, growing trade and financial linkages with the rest of the world can confer important benefits through investment and growth, but such linkages can also increase an economy's exposure to spillovers from abroad. Furthermore, Cambodia's underlying vulnerabilities can amplify the impact of external shocks. For example, because the economy depends on a few sectors and concentrated exports, global price shocks can easily translate into relatively large terms of trade shocks and thus embody higher financial stability risks.[2] Cambodia's underlying vulnerabilities can be usefully illustrated schematically as the interaction between macroeconomic and structural vulnerabilities (IMF, 2011a), as in Figure 5.1.

[2]Beyond the real economy, financial shocks from capital flows appear to be the most pertinent risk for Cambodia. Since many banks in Cambodia can easily source funding from liquidity-rich Asian economies, as evidenced in recent quarters, the potential for surges in bank flows and associated risks remains high. Although dollarization and low debt may partly mitigate the risks of a currency and/or debt crisis, financial stability risks could still stem from a credit boom induced by bank flows, the most volatile of all capital flows (IMF, 2011b).

Figure 5.1

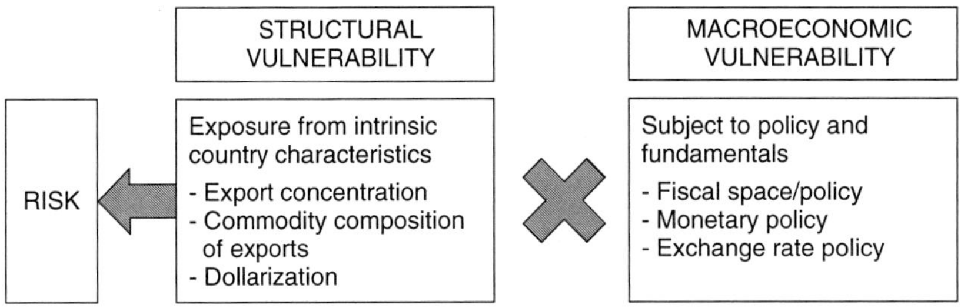

We will first underscore the features of the Cambodian economy that give rise to these structural and macroeconomic vulnerabilities and then stress their sectoral implications. We will also explore how the economic risks are likely to evolve amid ongoing trade and financial integration against the backdrop of Asia's economic rebalancing.

SOURCES OF VULNERABILITY: STRUCTURAL AND MACROECONOMIC

This section highlights the key sources of vulnerabilities for Cambodia and groups them into *structural* and *macroeconomic* factors. It should be noted that these two groups of factors are often interlinked and therefore jointly determine the overall vulnerabilities.

Structural Sources of Vulnerability

Production structure. Cambodia's economic base remains narrow. For example, its merchandise production base is still concentrated and exposed to external shocks, as evidenced by the sharp growth slowdown in 2009 following the onset of the global financial crisis.[3]

Export structure. Exports remain heavily concentrated, with garments and footwear accounting for more than 80 percent of merchandise exports (Figure 5.2). Early signs of export diversification through commodities—rice, rubber, and a few other agricultural commodities—and non-textile manufacturing (e.g., recent Japanese investments in light manufacturing such as automotive supplies) are slowly emerging, though from a very low base.

[3]Among the 64 low-income countries surveyed by the IMF (2010), the decline in average growth between 2007 and 2009 was 2.8 percentage points (from 6.0 percent to 3.2 percent). Cambodia exerienced the second largest growth collapse, behind only Georgia.

Figure 5.2 Concentrated Export Structure

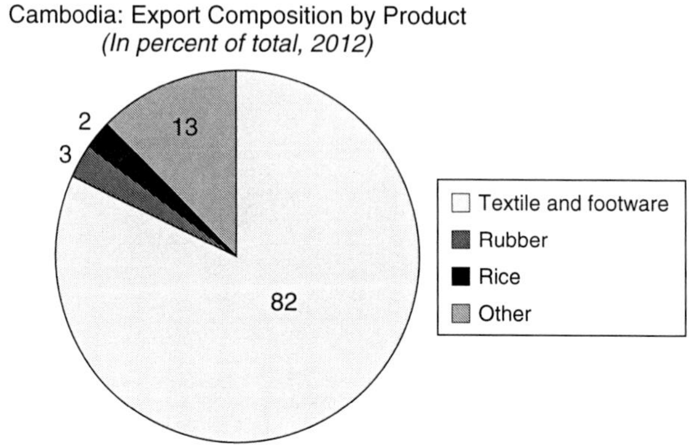

Source: Data provided by the Cambodian authorities.

Figure 5.3 Market Diversification

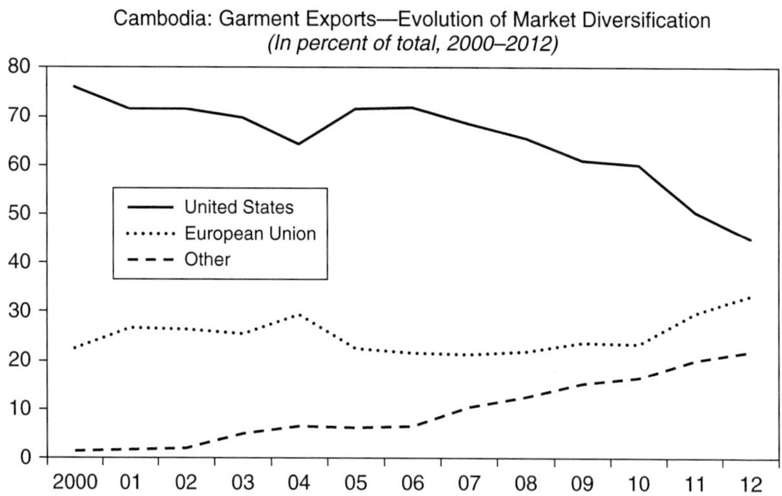

Source: Data provided by the Cambodian authorities.

Export market. Export market diversification is under way, beginning with the recent headway that Cambodian textiles have made into European (catalyzed by preferential access) and other markets, such as Japan, reducing the country's exclusive reliance on the U.S. market for export growth. But, as illustrated by Figure 5.3, market diversification is taking place only gradually.

Dollarization. Cambodia has one of the highest levels of dollarization relative to its peers, including within the region (Figure 5.4). Empirical evidence suggests that dollarization can increase the vulnerability of a country's financial system by increasing its solvency and liquidity risks (Gulde and others, 2004). Cross-country

Figure 5.4 Cross-Country Comparison of Dollarization

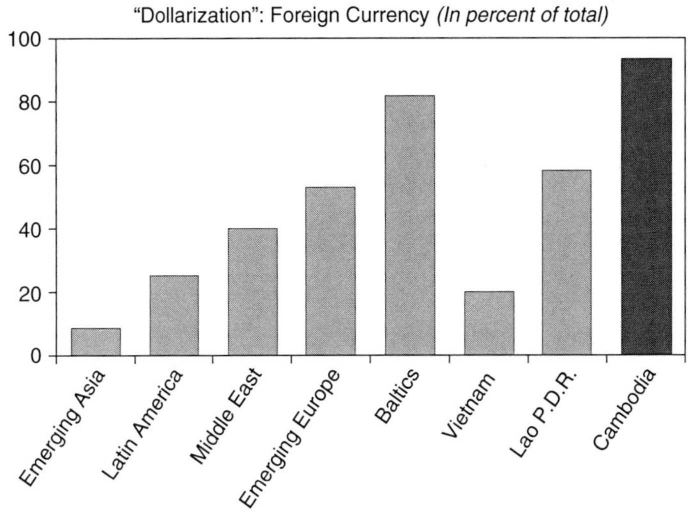

Source: Ranciere, Tornell, and Vamvakidis (2010).

estimates of the impact of dollarization on some key indicators of financial soundness, while controlling for changes in underlying macroeconomic volatilities, are consistent with the hypothesis that a rise in dollarization may increase financial vulnerability. In particular, the variance of deposit growth is positively correlated with the degree of dollarization, suggesting that highly dollarized financial systems may be more exposed to credit cycles and liquidity risk, given their limited control over monetary policy and liquidity management tools.

Shallow or missing financial market and safety net. A confluence of factors hampers risk management in the financial system and, in turn, accentuates financial fragilities in Cambodia. The main factors include (i) a lack of government securities, resulting in the absence of any lower-risk instruments in the system to support interbank market activity; and (ii) a shallow and informal foreign exchange market.[4] The lack of a well-developed interagency crisis management framework and a deposit insurance system could accentuate a banking crisis.

Banking system structure. Cambodia's banking system is highly liberalized and dollarized. In addition, foreign banks have a large presence, representing more than two-thirds of all banks and accounting for half of total deposits. As discussed in Chapter 4 of this volume, the banking system appears to be overbanked, populated by a large cluster of small banks.[5] At the same time, it is relatively

[4]The shallow foreign exchange market can come under pressure (in either direction) from sizable transactions, as partly foreshadowed when the first listed stock started trading in the Cambodian Stock Exchange in 2012.

[5]A few specialized banks are restricted from taking domestic deposits.

concentrated, with the five largest banks directly controlling about 60 percent of banking system assets at end-2012. The proliferation of banks could weaken financial stability, including by encouraging excessive risk taking, limiting the scope for product diversification, and overburdening supervisory capacity as the system relies more on foreign funding. In addition, cross-country evidence actually suggests a negative correlation between the number of banks and the degree of competition between them (Claessens and Laeven, 2004).

Quasi-banking activities. Microfinance institutions are growing rapidly in Cambodia and increasing their presence in banking services, with their total assets at 10 percent of GDP at end-2012. Their capital structure makes them particularly exposed to funding shocks, with about three-fourths of their funding sourced from abroad, so shocks could cause spillover into the banking system given their increasing interconnectedness.[6]

Macroeconomic Sources of Vulnerability

Shifting sources of external demand. Cambodia's growth has exhibited strong and increasing co-movements with the United States, the European Union, and emerging Asia.[7] The degree of correlation between Cambodia and other countries and regions has increased substantially during the last decade (Figure 5.5). Reflecting ongoing trade and financial integration, Cambodia's growth in recent years has been increasingly driven by external factors, including from Asia.

Sectorally, the intensifying integration with Asia has taken place through trade and tourism. Among the most notable trends in Cambodia, imports from

Figure 5.5 Cambodia's Growing Economic Integration by Region

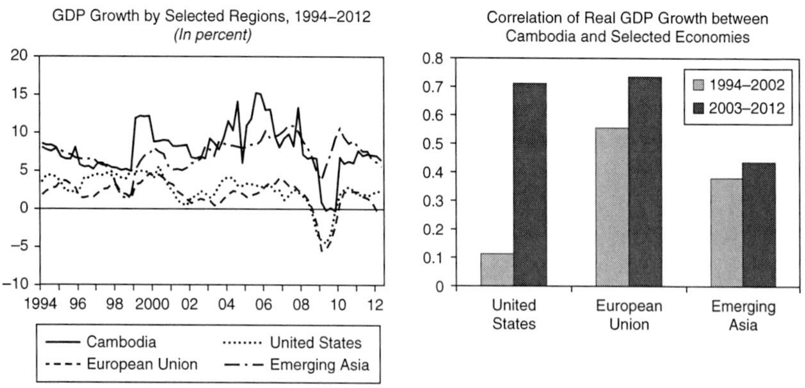

Source: IMF, World Economic Outlook (WEO) database (October 2012); and IMF staff calculations.

[6]It should be noted that in recent years microfinance institutions have increasingly been shifting their funding strategy toward domestic deposits.

[7]Emerging Asia refers to China, Hong Kong SAR, India, Indonesia, the Republic of Korea, Malaysia, the Philippines, Singapore, Taiwan Province of China, Thailand, and Vietnam.

Figure 5.6 Evolving Sources of External Demand in Cambodia

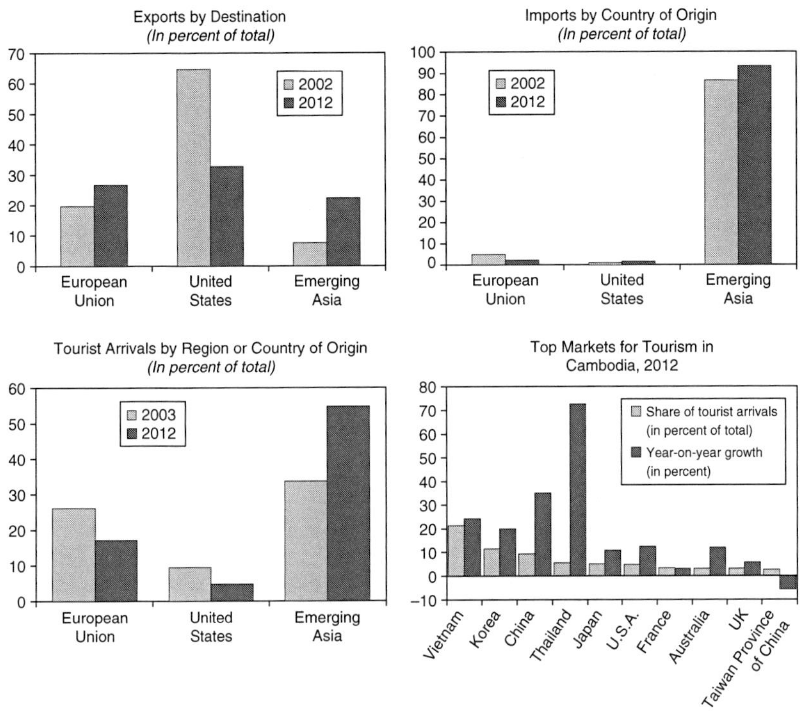

Sources: CEIC Asia database (bottom panels); and IMF, Direction of Trade Statistics database (top panels).

emerging Asia are the highest of all the regions and continue to rise steadily, while imports from the United States and the European Union have changed marginally, a development that goes beyond textiles and holds even after controlling for exports to China. Even though exports to emerging Asia are still relatively modest, that region's share has more than tripled during the past 10 years, while during the same period the share of tourist arrivals from emerging Asia has almost doubled, reaching 55 percent in 2012 (Figure 5.6).

Growth spillovers. Box 5.1 highlights the empirical finding that external shocks are playing an increasingly large role in explaining growth volatility in Cambodia, with Asia becoming the source of an increasing share of spillovers. Econometric analysis also confirms the rising importance of emerging Asia in recent years (Box 5.2). Although historical spillover estimates for the euro area remain modest, such spillovers in Cambodia are likely to increase in the years ahead, given increasing trade flows and preferential tariff agreements, especially in the garment exporting sector.

Limited fiscal space. With a tax-to-GDP ratio at around 12 percent, Cambodia's revenue performance remains weak by the standards of both its region and other peer economies, mainly reflecting administrative weaknesses (see Chapters 6 and 7).

BOX 5.1

Decomposing Cambodia's Growth Volatility

Variance decomposition analysis captures how much of the variation in economic activity can be explained by external shocks. External shocks contributed to 40 percent of the variation in Cambodia's economic activity between 1994 and 2012 and to 60 percent of it during the last decade. The United States remains the single most important external source of business cycle variation (or economic swings) in Cambodia, accounting for 20 percent of the economic variation explained by external shocks during the whole sample period (1994–2012), and doubling its contribution during the past decade. Similarly, emerging Asia, which was responsible for 14 percent of economic variation over the whole sample period, is an increasing source of variation, accounting for 20 percent of Cambodia's economic swings over the past decade.

Figure 5.1.1

Contribution to Variation in Growth *(In percent)*

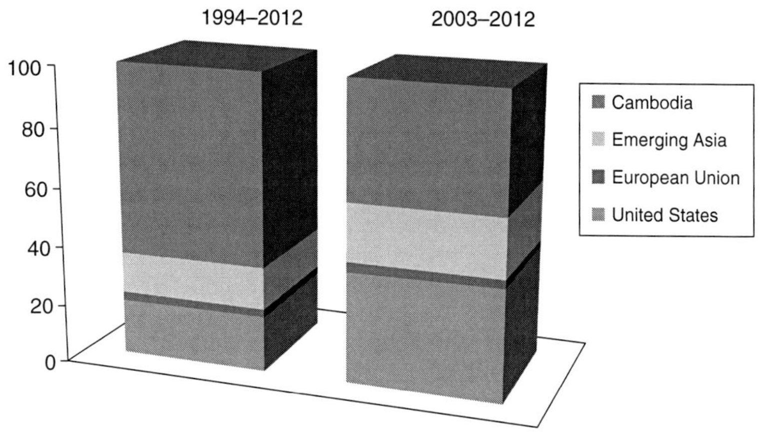

Sources: IMF, *International Financial Statistics*, 2012; and IMF staff calculations.

After stalling for some time, revenue performance improved in 2012 owing to economic buoyancy and strengthened administration. Contingent liabilities from the financial sector and government guarantees to hydropower projects also constrain fiscal space.

Low level of government deposits. In the aftermath of the global financial crisis, the stock of government deposits, the only readily available fiscal buffer for Cambodia, declined to about 4 percent of GDP in 2012 from 8 percent of GDP (precrisis). These deposits serve as an important policy buffer in the absence of

BOX 5.2

Growth Spillover Analysis for Cambodia

To evaluate growth spillovers from external shocks, a vector autoregressive (VAR) model is used. The analysis focuses on the impact of shocks to real GDP growth in the United States, the European Union, and emerging Asia on Cambodia's real GDP growth during 1994:Q1–2012:Q2, with the sources of spillovers measured and ranked by a Cholesky ordering as follows: the United States, the European Union, and emerging Asia. Changes in ordering did not yield significantly different results.

The main results are as follows:

- The United States remains the main source of growth spillover for Cambodia: a one percentage point deviation of the U.S. GDP growth rate from its mean leads to a one percentage point deviation in Cambodia's growth.
- Growth spillover from emerging Asia has a significant and growing impact on Cambodia. A one percentage point deviation in emerging Asia's growth from its mean leads to a 0.9 percentage point deviation in Cambodia's growth.
- The impact of emerging Asia's growth spillover has also increased in the past decade (2003–12). A one percentage point deviation in that region's growth from its mean causes a 1.4 percentage point deviation in Cambodia's growth.

Figure 5.2.1 Impulse Response Function: One Percent Shock from Selected Economies
(Percentage change in mean deviation)

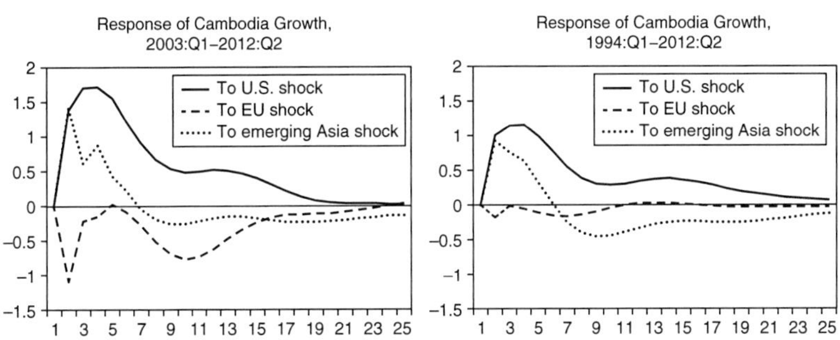

Source: IMF staff calculations.

government domestic debt, with their reconstitution requiring fiscal consolidation.

Constrained exchange rate and monetary policy framework. High dollarization constrains both monetary and foreign exchange policy (see Chapter 3). One of the side effects has been the stunted development of a formal foreign exchange market. Although dollarization in the wake of the post-conflict reconstruction phase imposed some policy discipline, the cost has been the lack of an independent monetary policy and use of the exchange rate to facilitate adjustment.

SECTORAL VULNERABILITIES

This section provides an aggregate view of the interaction of *sectoral* vulnerabilities—external, financial, and fiscal—with the *structural* and *macroeconomic* vulnerabilities described above. Given Cambodia's concentrated production structure, limited fiscal space, and high dollarization, sectoral vulnerabilities are quite interlinked. For example, a credit boom amid high dollarization and limited exchange rate flexibility can increase both financial and external sector vulnerabilities. In fact, rapid credit growth and the accompanying domestic demand boom in a stabilized or fixed exchange rate regime can lead to larger current account deficits and raise external sustainability risks. Additionally, external shocks, such as a reversal of capital flows, can worsen financial stability risks given the openness of the banking system and capital account.

External Sector

Traditional (and often backward-looking) indicators suggest that Cambodia's vulnerability to the external sector is relatively benign. The import coverage of its reserves was around 4½ months at end-2012; its short-term external debt is low; and Bank for International Settlements (BIS) data show that cross-border banking sector exposure is limited (see Figure 5.7).[8] But, as noted above, external vulnerability is closely linked to financial sector vulnerability. As a result, the rapidly transforming financial sector and sharp changes in Cambodia's debt (both public and private) profile could have a bearing on medium-term external vulnerability.

The lessons for Cambodia from emerging Europe are instructive in this regard. Emerging Europe experienced rapid foreign-currency-denominated credit growth, a large presence of foreign banks, a credit-fueled domestic demand boom, and large current account deficits, but ultimately faced external crises when the cycle reversed. As discussed in Chapter 4, Cambodia remains structurally poised to face similar types of vulnerability, since some of the ingredients for external vulnerabilities are in place or could emerge quickly. For example, recent credit growth in Cambodia has been accompanied by increasing bank flows from abroad. It is important to note that many of these risks are often underestimated during an economic upswing.

Financial Sector

Credit growth is one of the most significant predictors of financial vulnerabilities and subsequent crises (Dell'Ariccia and others, 2012). Cambodia now has one of the highest rates of credit growth in Asia (Figure 5.8), primarily in foreign currency and from a modest base (Box 5.3). With a credit-to-GDP ratio at over 35 percent,

[8]BIS cross-border exposure statistics do not include banks from Cambodia's neighbors such as China and Vietnam, which have recently become more active.

Figure 5.7 Cross-Border Banking Sector Exposure to Cambodia

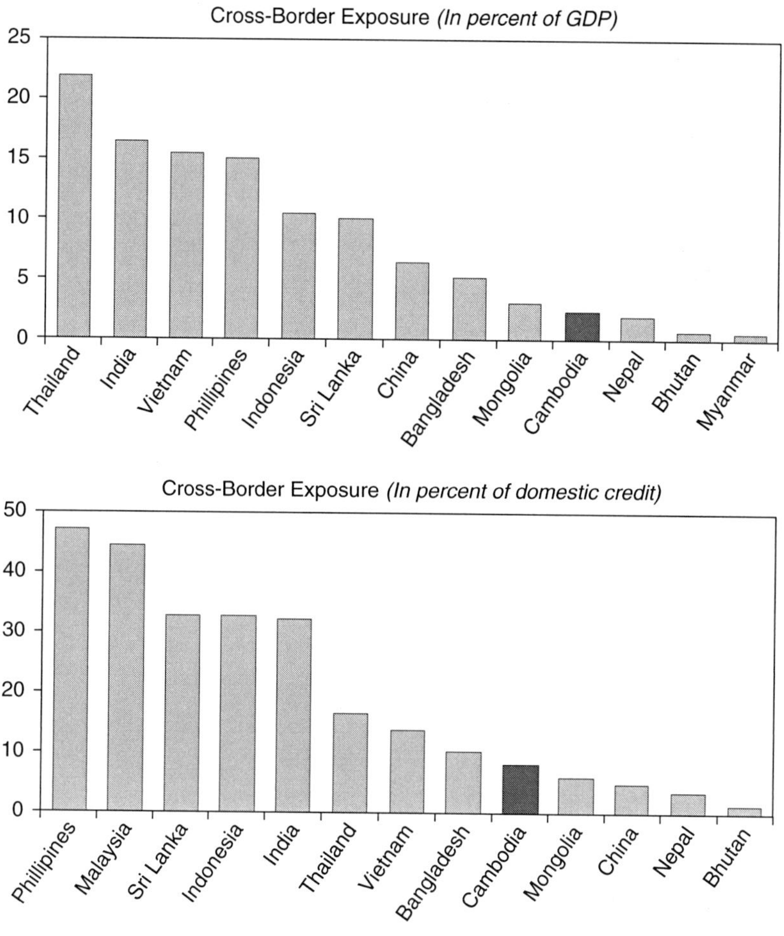

Sources: Bank for International Settlements; and IMF, World Economic Outlook database (April 2012).

the size of the banking system, as a share of GDP, is already bigger than in some emerging Asian economies, such as Indonesia and the Philippines (Figure 5.9).[9]

To provide a regional and historical perspective, Cambodia's credit growth, at over 30–35 percent, is far higher than that of its regional peers when they experienced comparable rapid growth (Figure 5.9). Moreover, the size of Cambodia's banking system relative to GDP is already larger than in other Asian economies during their economic takeoffs in the 1970s and 1980s. Going

[9]It is important to point out that other indicators, for example the size and activity of capital markets—equity and debt—are still very rudimentary or nonexistent (debt), pointing to a still maturing financial system.

BOX 5.3

When Is Credit Growth Too Fast? (And How to Deal With It)

Cambodia's financial system appears to be shifting from a normal deepening to excessive credit growth. Cambodia's financial system is expanding rapidly. With private credit growing by more than 30 percent during 2012–13, the credit-to-GDP ratio has reached 37 percent, well above the median for low-income countries. If credit growth were to continue at the current pace, by end-2013 the ratio would exceed even the median for more advanced emerging market economies. These benchmarks suggest that the size of Cambodia's financial system has already outstripped the level that can be justified by normal financial deepening.[1]

Figure 5.3.1

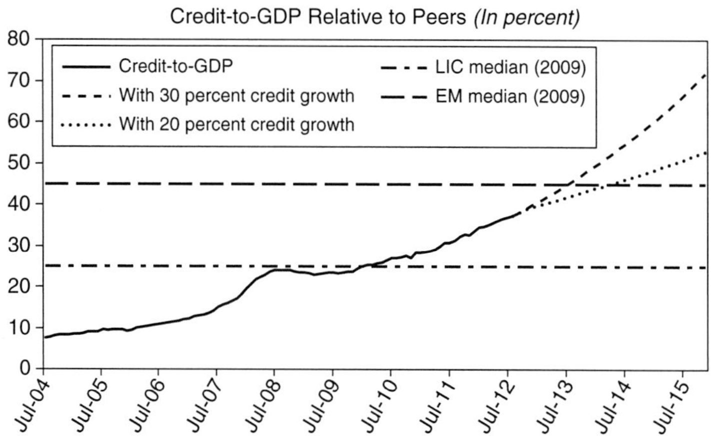

Sources: Cambodian authorities; and IMF staff estimates and projections.
Note: EM = emerging market; LIC = low-income country.

Cambodia's past trend of credit-to-GDP ratio is another simple proxy for the normal pace of financial deepening. To the extent that the actual credit-to-GDP ratio deviates significantly from its trend, one might interpret it as a sign of overheating in the credit market. This "credit gap" measure has indeed been empirically shown to be a good predictor of financial stress.[2] At 30 percent credit growth, the gap measure would widen rapidly and by end-2013 surpass a level last seen in 2008 at the height of Cambodia's real estate boom, which ended in a bust. Projecting this expansion further shows that Cambodia's credit trajectory is clearly breaking away from the country's own long-term pace of financial deepening.

Macroprudential measures may be needed. In addition to raising the reserve requirement, currently the only tool at the disposal of the National Bank of Cambodia, consideration should be given to other macroprudential measures. At its current level, the reserve requirement is not binding on most Cambodian banks, since they still possess considerable excess liquidity. As a result, a number of them have lowered interest rate spreads in recent years to compete for market share. Some are also increasingly relying on cheaper external funding from foreign banks, with commercial banks' other

Figure 5.3.2

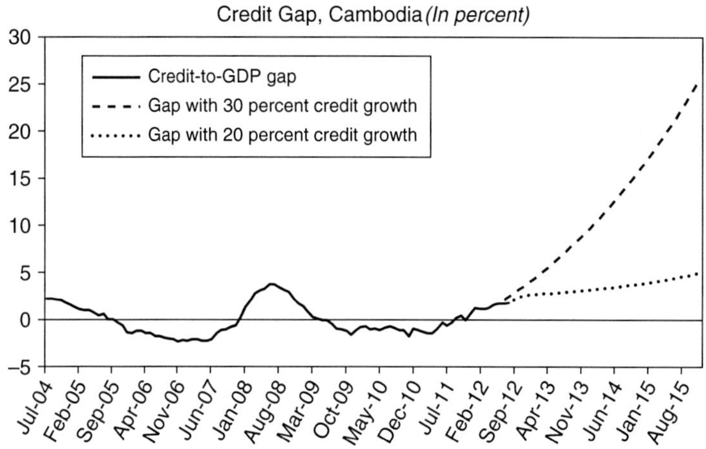

Sources: Cambodian authorities; and IMF staff estimates and projections.

foreign liabilities tripling in 2012 and nonresident deposits increasing fivefold since 2009 (albeit from a low base).

What measures and trade-offs? In considering macroprudential measures, the National Bank of Cambodia must strike a balance in choosing an instrument that is not only simple to implement but also effective in slowing credit growth and causes the least distortions to the credit market. For example, adopting a capital surcharge would be relatively simple and create few distortions, but it might be less effective in an already booming credit market, where capital has been boosted by profitability. Also, the capital-to-asset ratio of 29 percent reported by Cambodian banks is already much higher than the regional average. On the other hand, a tightening of the loan-to-value cap, while potentially effective, could be complicated by challenges in asset valuations. Capping the loan-to-deposit ratio, which rose to 89 percent in 2012 from 82 percent at end-2010, could also be effective, but it would have a disproportionate impact on foreign bank branches that rely less on their deposit base, potentially causing distortions to competition.

[1]The benchmarks are taken from IMF (2012a), based on global samples of 35 low-income countries and 108 emerging market economies.
[2]See Borio and Drehmann, 2009.

beyond individual country comparisons, Cambodia's credit-to-GDP ratio now is far above the median for low-income countries and, at the current pace of growth, will soon exceed the median among emerging market economies as well. This too highlights the need for regulatory vigilance (Box 5.3). As noted earlier, high dollarization significantly limits the central bank's ability to curb credit growth and minimize financial stability risks. Therefore, large external

Figure 5.8 Cross-Country Comparison of Credit Growth *(In precent, year-over-year, 2012:Q1)*

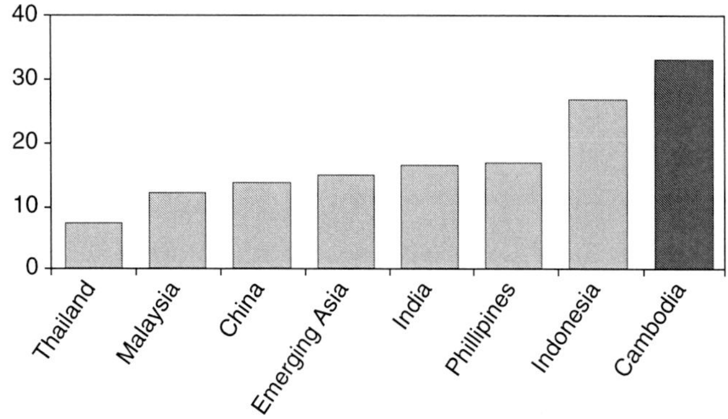

Source: IMF staff calculations.

Figure 5.9 Comparing Cambodia's Financial Depth and Credit Growth *(Financial Depth of Regional Peers at Economic Takeoff and Credit Growth During the Boom Years)*

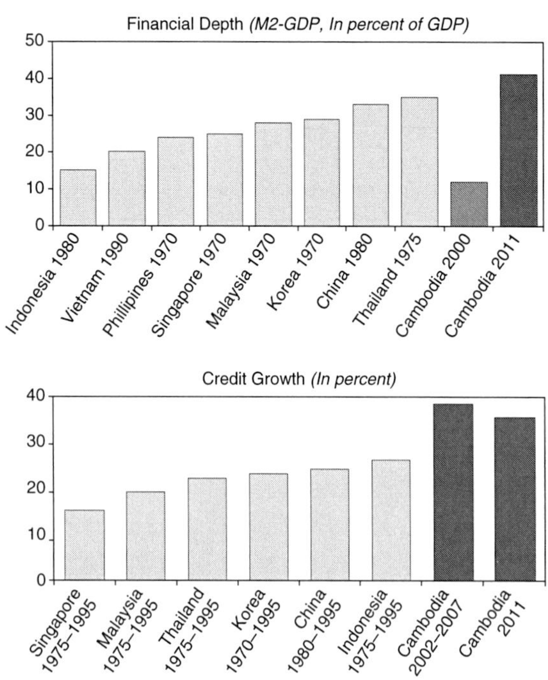

Sources: World Bank, World Development Indicators; and IMF staff calculations.

shocks and consequent macroeconomic vulnerability can easily translate into financial sector vulnerability and further amplify negative feedback loops between these two sectors.

Fiscal Vulnerabilities

Fiscal vulnerabilities stem from both structural and macroeconomic factors: (i) low-revenue; (ii) risks from contingent liabilities (e.g., government guarantees); and (iii) the role of fiscal policy as the main policy lever in case of large shocks. The low level of government deposits, the key fiscal buffer in the absence of a government securities market, further constrains the potency of fiscal policy to respond to adverse shocks.

THE IMPACT OF ASIA'S REBALANCING

Asia's rebalancing—the ongoing shift in the region from export-led to domestic demand-led growth, in part spurred by the slow recovery in advanced economies—will in the years ahead deeply transform many facets of regional economic relations. As a result of the 2008–09 global financial crisis, many advanced economies will have to save more as they deleverage and repair their private and public balance sheets. Increasingly, the growth in the counterpart economies that relied on exports and financed advanced economies (e.g., current account surplus economies in Asia such as China) will have to be increasingly driven by domestic demand, resulting in higher imports. These cross-currents—slower growth in traditional export destinations in advanced economies but stronger final demand from emerging Asia, especially China (Box 5.4)—will not only open up new opportunities for frontier economies such as Cambodia but also will likely alter the sources and magnitude of risks.

For Cambodia, the broader rebalancing trend in Asia is best captured through the prism of China's rebalancing, which has three facets: (i) as a source of regional final demand, (ii) as a supply chain hub, and (iii) as a competitor. Cambodia's medium-term productive capacity will likely continue to consist of commodity production and labor-intensive manufacturing, making the first two facets of China's rebalancing more relevant. With this rebalancing taking place against the backdrop of an industrial upgrading and rising regional wages, Cambodia's attractiveness as an investment destination has the potential to improve (IMF, 2012b).

The transmission channels of spillover from China's rebalancing would include, among other things, (i) trade, (ii) foreign direct investment, and (iii) capital flows—both portfolio flows (debt and equity) and other flows (e.g., bank flows). The capital flow channel, although currently modest, has the potential to increase sharply over the medium term as capital markets deepen and banks in Cambodia seek additional low-cost funding from abroad, including from their parent banks, some of which are located in Asian economies with liquidity surpluses. Finally, official loans from China constitute the single largest source of external public donor financing in Cambodia (Box 5.4).

BOX 5.4

Cambodia's Scope for Regional Integration as Asia, Especially China, Rebalances

Asia's rebalancing will affect both the direction and strength of Cambodia's economic integration with the region and the global economy. By some measures, Cambodia is already well integrated with Asia: 67 percent of foreign direct investment and about 70 percent of imports come from emerging Asia. But Asia's rebalancing will likely significantly increase exports to emerging Asia, now at only 20 percent of total, and capital flows. The creation of the ASEAN Economic Community will further accentuate that trend since Cambodia, as a hub, would attract investment to tap into the ASEAN market of 600 million people.

Going forward, consumption-led domestic demand in China is expected to witness a secular increase, underpinned by rising household income. In fact, even as the global financial crisis was unfolding, Chinese household consumption increased by 48 percent between 2008 and 2011—by 52 percent in urban areas and 35 percent in rural areas, in part supported by a government policy of increasing basic pensions, social transfers, and unemployment benefits.

China, with its ample liquidity, is already the largest provider of financial support and foreign direct investment to Cambodia, accounting for over two-thirds of bilateral loans and over 40 percent of foreign direct investment during 2006–12. Most of these loans were concessional and associated with development projects.

Figure 5.4.1

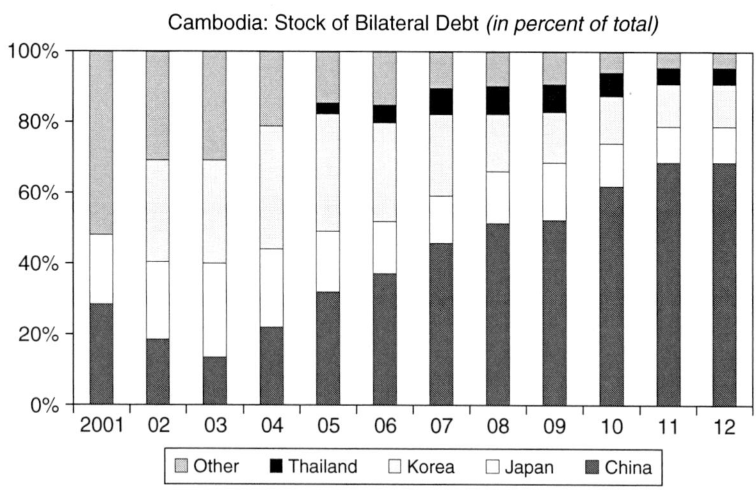

Source: Ministry of Economy and Finance, Cambodia.

Given Camobodia's limited access to global capital markets, these loans are an important source for the country's much needed infrastructure development.

At the industry level, higher wages (three to four times higher) in China are already catalyzing opportunities for Cambodia to expand its industrial base, initially in garments, but now increasingly in other labor-intensive manufacturing. More than 50 percent of the garment factories in Cambodia are from China and Taiwan Province of China.

A growing number of factories are now targeting the domestic market in China instead of the traditional advanced economies. Similar trends are emerging with respect to Japanese investments in Cambodia, which are catering to final demand in Japan (e.g., garments and commodities) and intermediate products for Japanese supply chains in other countries (e.g., Vietnam and Thailand). The upside potential of

Figure 5.4.2

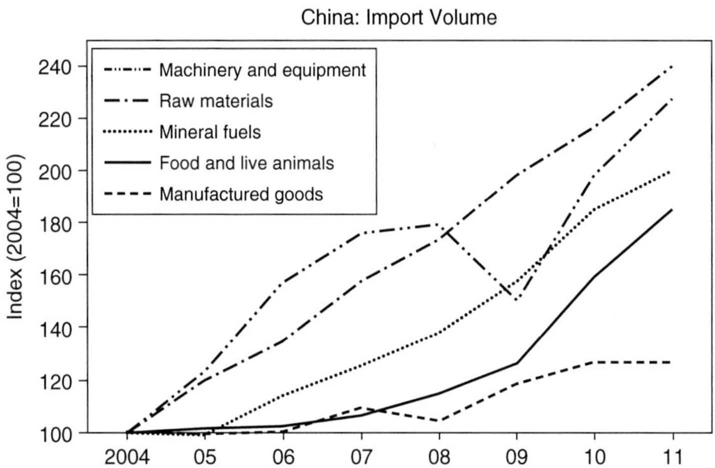

Source: National Bureau of Statistics of China.

Figure 5.4.3

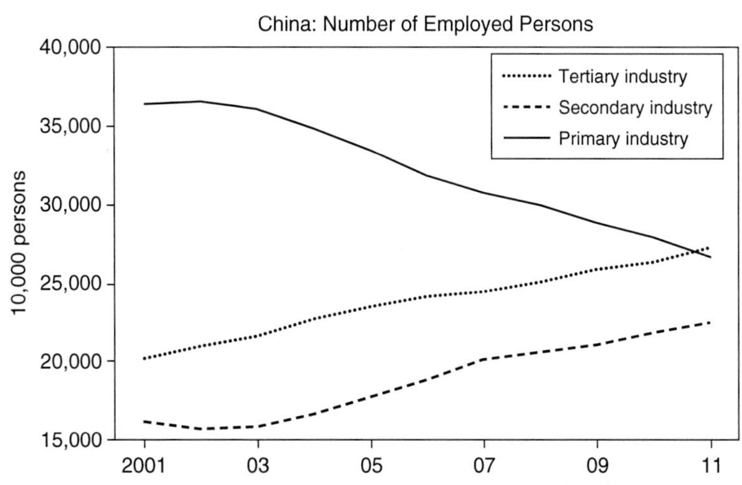

Source: National Bureau of Statistics of China.

(Continues on page 80)

BOX 5.4 (Continued)

the Chinese domestic market for Cambodia is highlighted by the pickup in exports to China, including manufactured products. Moreover, with continued urbanization and the rise of middle-income households in China and in other emerging Asian economies, the demand for agricultural products will increase, providing an opportunity for land-rich Cambodia to expand agro-processing industries. Similarly, the tourism sector is successfully pivoting toward the Asian market, with the share of tourist arrivals from emerging Asia almost doubling between 2003 and 2012, helping the industry to cope with the fallout from the recent financial crisis in the United States and the euro area.

This upside potential from China's rebalancing is subject to risks. Non-labor costs—such as electricity and transportation—are higher in Cambodia than in its regional peers. Despite significant progress in promoting growth over the past decade and improvements in the business climate, there is significant room for enhancing Cambodia's competitiveness relative to the region (see Table 5.4.1). The urgency of continued reform is highlighted by the fact that the potential labor supply for manufacturing is much smaller than in larger frontier economies such as Bangladesh and Myanmar. Furthermore, given the high level of dollarization in Cambodia, the prospects of a stronger dollar relative to other major currencies for the next few years increases the risks.

TABLE 5.4.1

Cambodia: Global Competitive Indices

Institutions	Year	Rating
UN, Human Development Index	2012	138/186
Heritage Foundation, Economic Freedom Index	2012	95/177
Transparency International, Corruption Perception Index	2012	157/176
World Bank, Ease of Doing Business Index	2012	133/185
World Economic Forum, Global Competitiveness Index	2012–13	85/144

In terms of vulnerabilities, therefore, a rotation of trade and finance toward emerging Asia, and China in particular, has the following implications for Cambodia.

Macroeconomic vulnerabilities. Structurally, the growing integration with emerging Asia could imply some diversification benefits as Cambodia broadens its economic base. However, these benefits in terms of vulnerability management will likely be limited to the extent that new trading partners and product groups are subject to similar shocks.

Financial sector vulnerabilities. The potential for risk buildup through capital flows is amplified as Cambodia further integrates with regional financial markets during Asia's rebalancing. In fact, some emerging market economies, such as China, are undergoing substantial financial sector reforms. The potential therefore remains high for financial risk spillovers (e.g., reversal of capital inflows) from unintended distortions created during the reform process. These spillover risks for Cambodia are compounded by the shallow capital and foreign exchange markets and the fact that the absolute size of its financial system is small compared to the size of the capital-exporting economies in the region.

Competitiveness. Cambodia will face increasing pressure to upgrade its infrastructure, human capital, and business environment as larger developing economies (e.g., Bangladesh and Myanmar) also compete for the same realm of export to emerging Asia.

RISKS AHEAD: STEPS TOWARD A MITIGATION STRATEGY

Cambodia is entering a new phase in transitioning from a low-income to an emerging-market economy. It is not only diversifying its economic base, but also adding new sources of risks to its existing structural vulnerabilities, as commonly experienced by regional emerging market economies during their economic takeoff. In this context, although Asia's rebalancing offers an exciting opportunity to improve the quality and increase the duration of that takeoff, the scope for vulnerability mitigation through diversification may be limited. Cambodia's economic vulnerabilities therefore need to be managed through a comprehensive approach, since its sectoral vulnerabilities can easily transmit from one sector to another (e.g., from the external to the financial sector). Asia's rebalancing might complicate the cross-sectoral transmission channel through similar shocks until financial markets deepen sufficiently and the economy becomes sufficiently diversified, highlighting the urgent need to build policy buffers in Cambodia.

Given that policy buffers are limited and can be built only gradually, a multipronged and forward-looking approach will be critical. The speed at which different buffers can be ramped up will also need to guide reform priorities. For example, since reducing structural vulnerabilities such as dollarization or diversifying the production base will take time, the burden of vulnerability mitigation will fall on stronger revenue efforts to build fiscal buffers and on better supervision to minimize financial stability risks. More specifically:

- ***Financial deepening.*** Financial deepening needs to be closely synchronized with market development (e.g., interbank and foreign exchange). Given the shifting funding structure of the banking system, moderating credit growth and closely monitoring risk buildup will need to be major components of the strategy to mitigate vulnerabilities.
- ***External buffers.*** External buffers, including the buildup of foreign exchange reserves and prudent external borrowing practices, need to be stepped up. Asia's rebalancing will likely accelerate Cambodia's integration with the global economy as an important growth driver, but it could also expose its economy to more external shocks.
- ***Fiscal buffers.*** Fiscal buffers need to be augmented by increasing revenue, replenishing government deposits, and minimizing contingent liabilities. These buffers also need to be commensurate with the elevated financial

sector risks as Cambodia matures into a full-fledged emerging market economy.

The recent literature points toward a virtuous cycle from the cross-sectoral synergy in a comprehensive strategy of vulnerability mitigation. First, policy buffers can reduce economic volatility. Second, reduced economic vulnerabilities support investment and economic growth and diversification. Third, export diversification also contributes to an acceleration of growth. Finally, prudent fiscal management and sound financial sector policies can reduce the cost of and increase access to funds for growth-friendly investment (e.g., in education and infrastructure) (Hesse, 2008; IMF, 2010).

Sustained and more resilient growth, in turn, will make it easier to build and safeguard policy buffers. A sound macro-financial environment, through the policies outlined above, can reduce macroeconomic and structural vulnerabilities and give rise to a self-sustaining vulnerability mitigation dynamic. Part II of this book takes a closer look at the package of policy measures—fiscal, monetary, and financial—that are important components of an overall risk management strategy in Cambodia's new phase of growth amid Asia's rebalancing and an ever changing global economic environment.

CONCLUSION

Cambodia's structural vulnerabilities stem from its concentrated production and export structure, its high degree of dollarization, and the limited development of its financial system, all against the backdrop of a deliberate strategy of maintaining an open economy. The key points that emerged from the analysis in this chapter may be summarized as follows.

- Cambodia's *macroeconomic* vulnerabilities reflect its structural vulnerabilities and initial conditions: a rapidly growing and increasingly interconnected financial system, limited monetary policy tools and exchange rate flexibility, and narrow fiscal space.
- Risk buildup from the interaction of *structural* and *macroeconomic* vulnerabilities during economic takeoff from a low-income to an emerging market economy can be rapid.
- To simultaneously address Cambodia's existing structural and macroeconomic vulnerabilities and additional vulnerabilities that may arise from their interaction, a comprehensive cross-sectoral approach to policy formulation will be needed. For example, safeguarding financial stability at the current juncture would not only require moderating credit growth, but also require further strengthening financial sector supervision, building more financial market infrastructure, and increasing policy buffers.
- Asia's rebalancing could offer some diversification benefits as Cambodia broadens its economic base, but in terms of managing vulnerabilities these benefits will likely be limited to the extent that new trading partners and product groups are subject to similar shocks.

REFERENCES

Borio, Claudio, and Mathias Drehmann, 2009, "Assessing the Risk of Banking Crises—Revisited," *BIS Quarterly Review*, March, pp. 29–46.

Claessens, Stijn, and Luc Laeven, 2004, "What Drives Bank Competition? Some International Evidence," *Journal of Money, Credit and Banking*, Vol. 36, No. 3, pp. 563–83.

Dell'Ariccia, Giovanni, Deniz Igan, Luc Laeven, and Hui Tong, 2012, "Policies for Macrofinancial Stability: How to Deal with Credit Booms," IMF Staff Discussion Note No. 12/06 (Washington: International Monetary Fund).

Gulde Anne-Marie, David Hoelscher, Alain Ize, David Marston, and Gianni De Nicolo, 2004, "Financial Stability in Dollarized Economies," IMF Occasional Paper No. 230 (Washington: International Monetary Fund).

Hesse, Heiko, 2008. "Export Diversification and Economic Growth," Commission on Growth and Development Working Paper No. 21 (Washington: World Bank).

International Monetary Fund, 2010, "Emerging from the Global Crisis–Macroeconomic Challenges Facing Low-Income Countries," Public Information Notice No. 10/148 (Washington: International Monetary Fund).

———, 2011a, "Managing Volatility: A Vulnerability Exercise for Low-Income Countries," IMF Policy Paper (Washington).

———, 2011b, "International Capital Flows, Reliable or Fickle?" Chapter 4 in *World Economic Outlook* (Washington, April).

———, 2012a, "Enhancing Financial Sector Surveillance in Low-Income Countries: Financial Deepening and Macro-Stability," IMF Policy Paper (Washington).

———, 2012b, *Regional Economic Outlook: Asia and Pacific* (Washington, April).

Loayza, Norman, Romain Rancière, Luis Servén, and Jaume Ventura, 2007, "Macroeconomic Volatility and Welfare in Developing Countries," *World Bank Economic Review*, Vol. 21, No. 3.

Ranciere, Roman, Aaron Tornell, and Athanasios Vamvakidis, 2010, "Currency Mismatch, Systemic Risk and Growth in Emerging Europe," *Economic Policy*, Vol. 25, No. 64, pp. 597–658.

Tabova, Alexandra, 2009, "Business Cycle Fluctuations in Low-Income Countries," unpublished paper, Duke University.

PART II

New Policies for Broader-Based Growth

CHAPTER 6

First Things First: Creating and Safeguarding Fiscal Space

TUBAGUS FERIDHANUSETYAWAN AND JOOKYUNG REE

In this chapter we describe Cambodia's main fiscal challenges and outline policy priorities over the near and medium term. The chapter focuses on three main issues: mobilizing revenue to rebuild fiscal space; managing public debt to safeguard that space and ensure fiscal and debt sustainability; and strengthening public financial management to improve the effectiveness of government spending. We provide cross-country comparisons to illustrate Cambodia's performance and the scope for improvement in the above areas relative to comparator countries in Asia.

THE FISCAL SETTING

Prudent fiscal policy and debt management serve as the bedrock of macroeconomic stability, given Cambodia's high degree of dollarization and the limited role of monetary policy. Since the process of dedollarization and the development of more effective monetary policy will take time, sound fiscal policy and debt management will continue to play a critical role in anchoring macroeconomic stability. Sound fiscal policy is also important to generate the resources needed to achieve long-term development objectives and promote more inclusive growth by improving equity and alleviating poverty. At the same time, sound public debt management will help ensure that the government's financing needs and its payment obligations are met at the lowest possible cost over the medium to long run, consistent with a prudent degree of risk. In fact, Cambodia's prudent public debt management has helped preserve macroeconomic stability for the past decade, although the rapidly growing contingent liabilities related to the development of large power projects will create new challenges in the future.

Cambodia's fiscal space—the room in its government budget to provide resources for fiscal policies—has declined substantially since 2009, and the progress of fiscal consolidation has been slow (Figure 6.1). Due to the absence of a market for government securities, government deposits serve as an important anchor for fiscal policy and as a buffer against shocks.[1] There was a rapid increase

[1]The fiscal buffers are also important since the central bank lacks a "lender of last resort" capacity and given the risk of a sudden stop in deposit flows due to banking system fragilities.

Figure 6.1 Fiscal Revenue and Government Deposits *(Percent of GDP)*

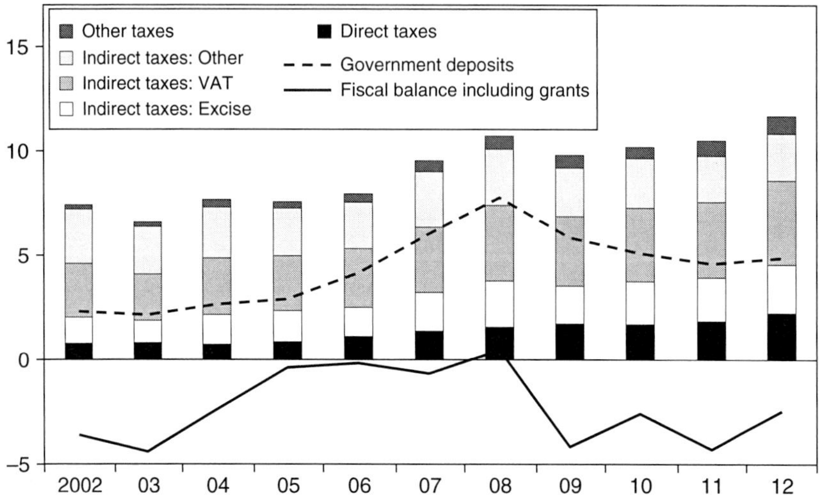

Sources: Cambodian authorities; and IMF staff estimates.

in government deposits during 2005–08, but the fiscal easing to mitigate the impact of the global financial crisis in 2008–09 used up a substantial part of this fiscal buffer. Cambodia has sought to rebuild government deposits since the crisis, but fiscal consolidation has been slow and the stock of government deposits relative to GDP continued to decline until 2011. Although revenue performance was exceptionally strong in 2012 and government deposits started to increase relative to GDP, the deposits remained at about 60 percent of their peak in 2008.

Against this background, continued fiscal consolidation over the medium term remains the top priority (Figure 6.2). Fiscal and debt management will need to strike a balance between: (i) rebuilding fiscal buffers through effective revenue mobilization; (ii) maintaining prudent current spending while providing enough resources for large development needs; and (iii) ensuring long-run public debt sustainability. To these ends, the government of Cambodia should

- continue to replenish the fiscal buffers in 2013 to lock in the gains from increased revenue received in 2012 and pave the way for further fiscal consolidation;
- implement a comprehensive revenue mobilization strategy to help achieve the goal under the Public Financial Management Reform Program (PFMRP) to raise domestic revenue by half a percentage point of GDP annually over the medium term;
- maintain broadly constant overall fiscal expenditure, relative to GDP, allowing the overall fiscal deficit to decline gradually by half a percentage point of GDP annually over the medium term and government deposits to rebound to 5–6 percent of GDP; and

Figure 6.2 Medium-Term Fiscal Outlook *(In percent of GDP)*

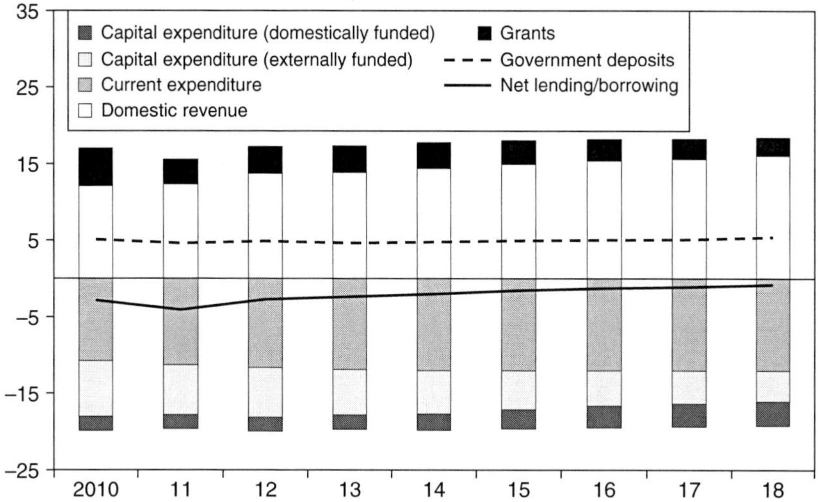

Sources: Cambodian authorities; and IMF staff estimates and projections.

- continue prudent debt management and careful management of fiscal risks by monitoring contingent liabilities to help safeguard fiscal space and preserve debt sustainability.

All these efforts need to be complemented by the consistent implementation of public financial management reforms both to improve the efficiency and equity of government spending and to strengthen governance. The remainder of this chapter discusses in greater detail the above fiscal challenges and policy priorities that Cambodia faces.

FISCAL CHALLENGES

Near-Term Challenges

Cambodia's main fiscal challenge in the near term is to rebuild its fiscal buffers, which have been running thin in the aftermath of the 2008–09 global financial crisis. Fiscal easing to support aggregate demand during the crisis was financed by external loans and a drawdown of government deposits. Despite a strong fiscal performance in 2012, progress in fiscal consolidation has been slow, partly because of weak revenue performance up to 2011 and partly because additional spending was needed to address the destructive floods in 2011. As a result, most of the buildup in fiscal buffers during the period of strong fiscal consolidation in 2005–08 was depleted. Government deposits continued to decline, falling from nearly 8 percent of GDP in 2008 to 4½ percent in 2011, before increasing to nearly 5 percent of GDP at end-2012 (Figure 6.3).

Figure 6.3 Government Deposits *(In percent of GDP)*

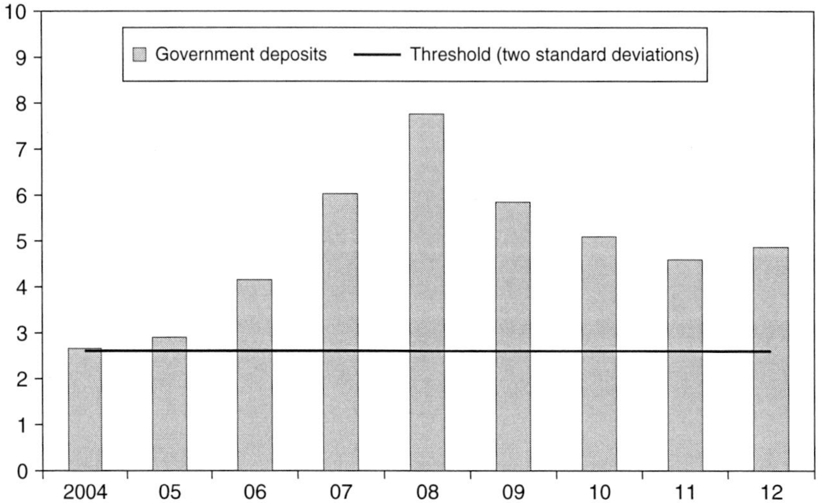

Sources: Cambodian authorities; and IMF staff estimates.

Although the stock of government deposits remains above the minimum level needed to withstand shocks, which is estimated at 2¾ percent of GDP,[2] fiscal space has become more limited. This reduction in Cambodia's fiscal buffers has important bearings on its vulnerability, particularly given the still fragile global recovery, subjecting Cambodia's economic outlook to considerable risks.

Medium-Term Challenges

Turning to medium-term challenges, Cambodia's fiscal revenue, particularly tax collection, remains low by regional standards (Figure 6.4). Tax revenue—at almost 11 percent of GDP during 2010–12—is much lower than that in other low-income countries, including those in the region, indicating a large scope for improvement. Cambodia has also relied more on indirect taxation (e.g., value-added tax (VAT), excise taxes, and trade taxes), which contributes to about 80 percent of total taxes, a rate much higher than the regional average of 60 percent. This suggests a need to focus on increasing collections from direct taxation, such as through income, profit, and wealth taxes.

Cambodia's tax regime is competitive, but there are various tax exemptions, all contributing to a generally low tax take. The VAT rate is 10 percent, slightly lower than the regional average of about 12 percent. Direct tax rates are also typically lower than regional averages, with the corporate tax rate at 20 percent as compared with a range of 25 to 30 percent in the rest of the region. The highest

[2]This is based on two standard deviations of government financing over 1995–2010, and thus fluctuations of the government's deficit related to the economic cycle.

Figure 6.4 Tax Revenue Indicators

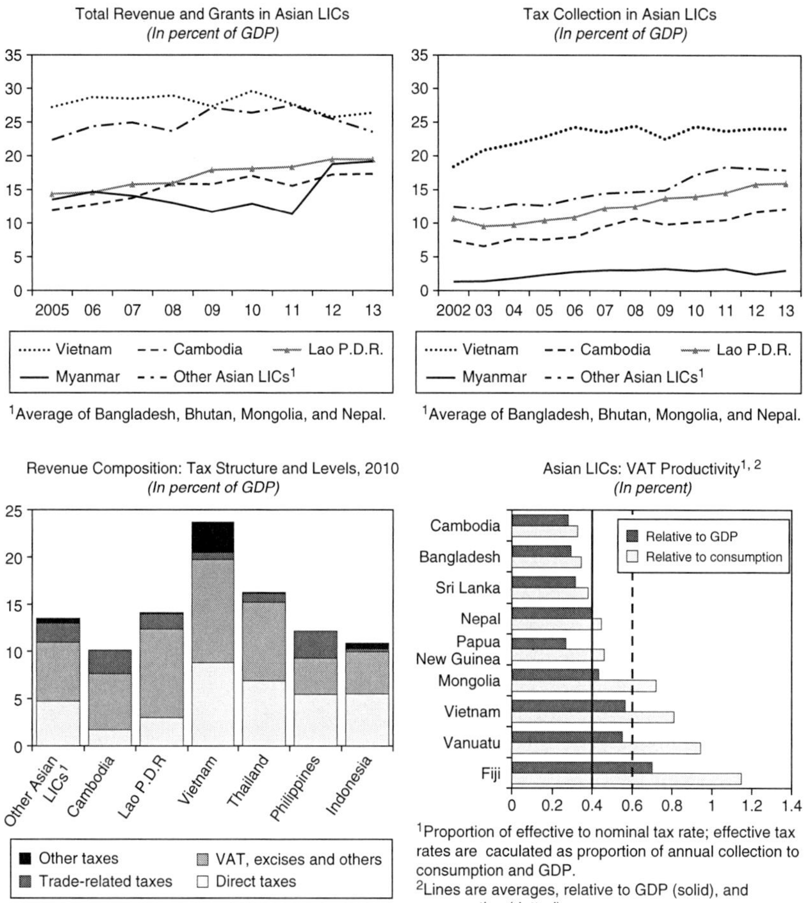

[1]Average of Bangladesh, Bhutan, Mongolia, and Nepal.

[1]Average of Bangladesh, Bhutan, Mongolia, and Nepal.

[1]Average of Bangladesh, Bhutan, Mongolia, Nepal, and Sri Lanka. 2009 data for Bangladesh and Bhutan, 2008 for Mongolia, 2011 for Nepal and Vietnam.

[1]Proportion of effective to nominal tax rate; effective tax rates are caculated as proportion of annual collection to consumption and GDP.
[2]Lines are averages, relative to GDP (solid), and consumption (dotted).

Sources: Country authorities; and IMF staff estimates.
Note: LICs = low-income countries; VAT = value added tax.

personal income tax rate is at 20 percent, compared with a range of 25 to 45 percent in the region. Like many other countries in the region, Cambodia provides several types of tax incentives, including income tax holidays and exemptions from VAT, import duties, and excises for qualified investment projects. Companies operating in its Special Economic Zones are also entitled to import duty exemptions for production equipment and inputs and construction materials. These tax incentives involve a loss of current and future revenue, create inefficiencies, and produce opportunities for tax abuse and corruption, especially in a country where policy implementation is fragmented and weak.

Improving Tax Revenue

Various indicators suggest that improving tax productivity and tax efforts could generate substantial revenue gains.[3] Estimates of the productivity of Cambodia's corporate income tax and VAT are at around 0.04 and 0.30, respectively, below the regional average of 0.15 and 0.45.[4] Another indicator of tax performance is *tax effort*, calculated as the actual tax collected relative to the estimated tax capacity, which is the maximum tax revenue for a country given its economic, social, institutional, and demographic characteristics. Cambodia's tax effort, estimated at 0.35, also falls short of the regional average of 0.50, suggesting that it could raise revenue by 6½–8 percent of GDP by aligning itself with the regional standards. This estimate is broadly consistent with another study, which shows that Cambodia's revenue-to-GDP ratio is about 5–7 percentage points below its potential (Box 6.1).

Although regional comparators provide only rough indicators and should be interpreted with caution, they suggest that by taking firm policy actions Cambodia could substantially increase revenue collection. They also indicate that while the scope for raising the tax yield is substantial, efforts will be needed in both tax policy reform and improved administration.

The pressure to increase revenue collection will become greater over time, as the base for trade taxes shrinks with the implementation of the ASEAN free trade area. Trade taxes, mostly in the form of import and export duties, contributed to about one-fifth of tax revenue during 2010–12. Since Cambodia is expected to eliminate its tariffs on goods imported from other ASEAN countries starting in 2015, the collection of trade taxes is projected to decline. However, the magnitude of this adverse impact is hard to estimate considering that the ASEAN free trade area trade preferences have been generally underutilized by ASEAN members, reflecting the costs of proving conformity with the rules of origin and uncertainties concerning the application of the system.

Further pressure on the revenue side arises from the fact that Cambodia has relied heavily on donor support, which is expected to decline over the medium term. Current and capital grants contributed to about one-fourth of total revenue in recent years, a substantially larger figure than the figure in comparator countries (Figure 6.5). This excludes other off-budget support, for example technical cooperation and assistance to nongovernmental organizations (NGOs). As Cambodia progresses toward middle-income status, donor support is expected to taper off, requiring the government to rely more on its own resources to meet development needs.

Composition of Spending

On the expenditure side, the composition of spending is comparable to that of other low-income countries in the region, although some challenges remain

[3]The estimates of tax performance indicators are taken from IMF (2011, 2012).

[4]This tax productivity measures the average yield in percent of GDP for each percentage point of the standard rates of corporate income tax and VAT. A low productivity indicates that various factors other than tax rates, such as tax incentives and low tax compliance, contribute to low revenue collection.

BOX 6.1

Revenue Norm Estimate for Cambodia

This box summarizes the findings from a regression-based analysis to estimate a revenue norm for Cambodia. The results indicate that Cambodia has considerable scope to increase revenues by aligning its revenue efforts with those of other low-income countries.

A cross-country comparison of revenue performance is analyzed by estimating a simple model linking a country's revenue-to-GDP ratio with its economic fundamentals, such as economic size and structure, level of development, and foreign direct investment. The sample consists of 49 low- and medium-income countries across the world spanning three observation years: 2001, 2005, and 2009. We estimate the following:

$$GGRN\_GDP_{\_it} = c + a \cdot \log(GPPC/ER_{\_it}) + b \cdot \log(GDP_{\_it}) + c \cdot \log(OILEXP_{\_it}) + d \cdot DI_{\_it} + e \cdot DI^{\wedge}2_{\_it} + u_{\_it}$$

where GGRN_GDP denotes the revenue (excluding grants) to GDP ratio; GPPC denotes GDP per capita; ER denotes the nominal exchange rate; GDP denotes the nominal GDP; OILEXP denotes oil exports; DI denotes direct investment; and DI^2 denotes direct investment squared (to allow for nonlinearities sometimes observed in the literature); with OILEXP and DI measured in U.S. dollars.

A pooled regression is estimated, with all explanatory variables statistically significant, while the signs of the estimated coefficients are broadly in line with expectations. Using these results, Figure 6.1.1 plots the estimated norm and the actual revenue-to-GDP ratio for all 49 countries in the sample in 2009, as represented by each diamond. Countries plotted above the 45 degree line are revenue underperformers relative to the norm, with Cambodia belonging to this group, given its actual revenue at 11.6 percent of GDP and its estimated norm at 16.8 percent. The figure also allows

Figure 6.1.1 Revenue to GDP Ratio: Norm vs. Actual
(In percent of GDP, 2009)

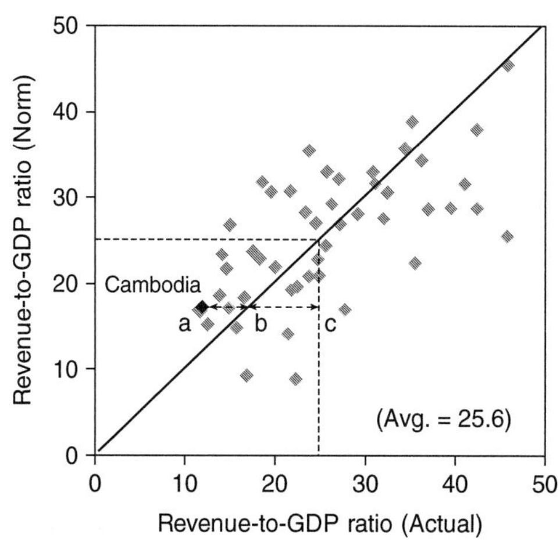

one to quantify the underperforming gap. Cambodia's actual performance is 14 percentage points lower than the group average at 25.6 percent (segment **a–c**), but a large fraction of this gap (8.8 percentage points, segment **b–c**) is from the difference between the group average and Cambodia's norm, representing Cambodia's relatively low income level, lack of natural resources, and limited foreign investment. The residual segment (5.2 percentage points, segment **a–b**) represents the gap between the actual and the norm, showing revenue underperformance that cannot be attributed to economic fundamentals and which likely comes from weak revenue administration and poor governance. For a robustness check, two alternative models (the first one omitting DI squared and the second one omitting both DI and DI squared) were estimated; they yielded broadly the same results, showing that Cambodia's revenue-to-GDP ratio is about 5 to 7 percentage points below its potential.

Figure 6.5 Grants to Asian Low-Income Countries *(In percent of total revenue)*

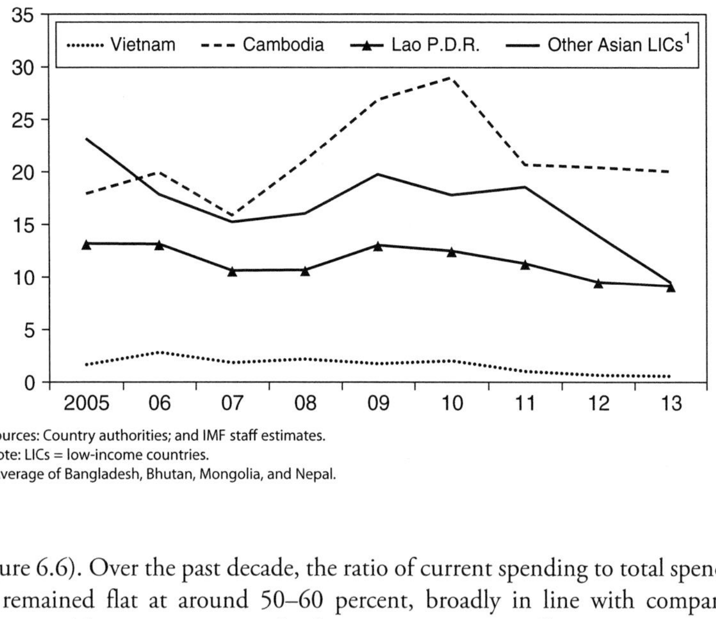

Sources: Country authorities; and IMF staff estimates.
Note: LICs = low-income countries.
[1]Average of Bangladesh, Bhutan, Mongolia, and Nepal.

(Figure 6.6). Over the past decade, the ratio of current spending to total spending has remained flat at around 50–60 percent, broadly in line with comparator countries. After increasing rapidly during 2005–09, overall current government spending has also remained flat in terms of GDP, partly reflecting prudent fiscal policies in view of the limited fiscal space available. The scope for spending increases will continue to be limited over the medium term unless the revenue target is met with a large margin.

Where Spending Reforms Are Needed

Regarding *current* spending, the wage bill has increased rapidly since 2009 in an effort to catch up with rising wages in the private sector. Cambodia's wage

Figure 6.6 Government Expenditure

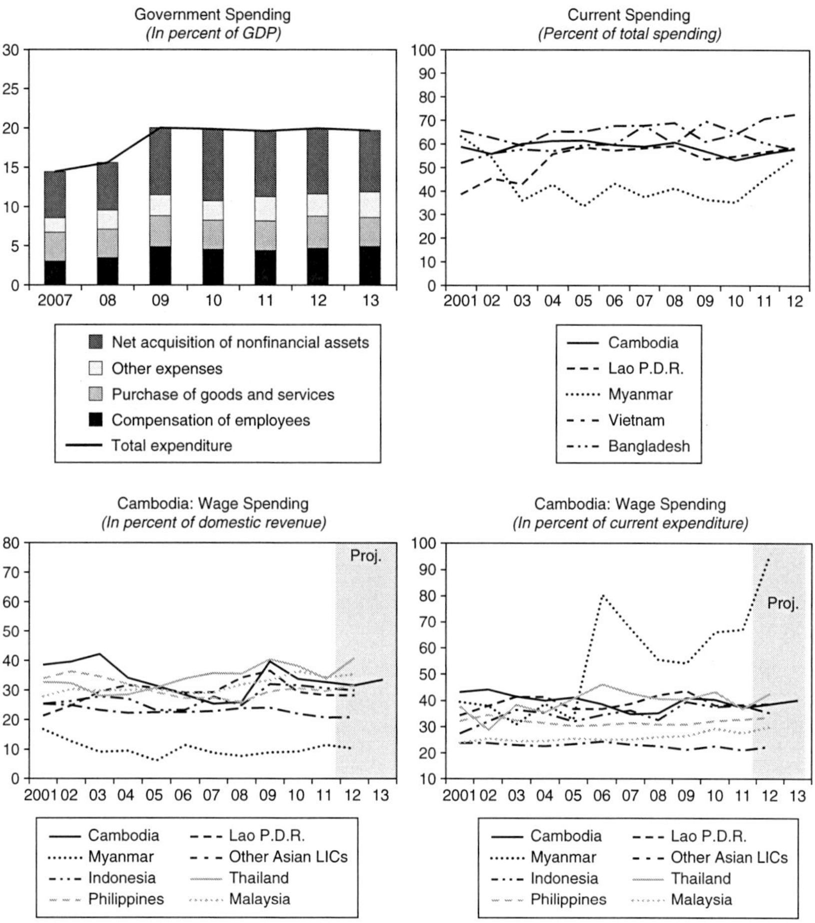

Source: Cambodian authorities; and IMF staff estimates.
Note: LICs = low-income countries; Proj. = projection.

bill, at about 4¾ percent of GDP in 2013, is broadly comparable with that in other Asian low-income countries, but as a share of domestic revenue and current expenditure, its burden is higher than for most comparator countries.

Regarding *capital* spending, the lack of a timely and detailed recording of outlays, particularly those financed by development partners, continues to hamper the planning and analysis of this spending. Donor support is not fully coordinated with the government and its implementation is not reported on a timely basis in the budget. Budget documents have so far included only aggregate estimates and the reporting has been fragmented. Better budget classification is critical, since classifying all donor projects as capital spending does not provide a clear

Figure 6.7 Goverment Spending in Priority Sectors *(In percent of GDP)*

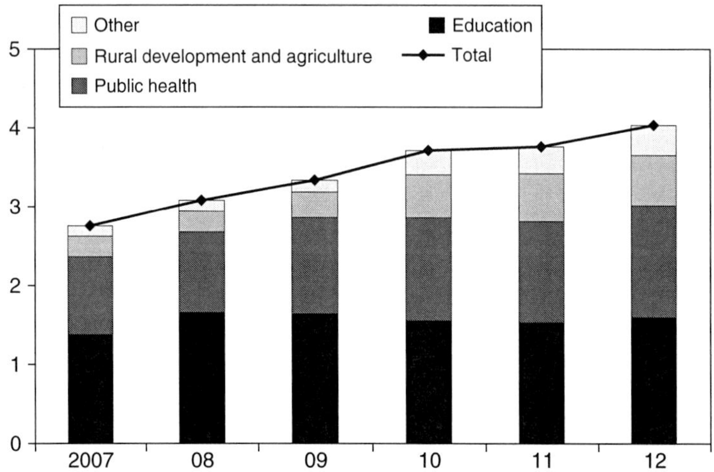

Sources: Cambodian authorities; and IMF staff estimates.

picture of development spending and therefore makes it difficult to plan and assess future development needs.

Spending on priority social sectors is largely in line with comparator countries, but spending efficiency could be improved (World Bank, 2011). The outcomes affected by public spending are also comparable, for example in terms of life expectancy, child mortality, primary school completion rates, and the ratio of girls to boys in school. Spending on agriculture and rural development (Figure 6.7) has continued to increase, and the level is broadly appropriate, but a complex set of structural constraints continues to hamper spending effectiveness and efficiency. These constraints include lack of continuity in public funding and poor rural infrastructure.

Therefore, the main challenge is to reallocate spending within the existing envelope, for example by providing more resources for agricultural research and extension services, secondary irrigation canals, and rural roads. Overall spending on health has also increased, although large out-of-pocket spending continues to put a burden on the poor. However, there are inefficiencies, for example, in the procurement of pharmaceuticals, medical equipment, and supplies, so that any larger allocation of certain health spending should be financed by savings within the sector. In the area of education, the main challenge is to improve efficiency by reallocating spending from primary education to higher levels of education.

Addressing Debt Sustainability

Cambodia's debt sustainability has improved, but foreign debt management remains a challenge, particularly in dealing with potentially large contingent liabilities

(Figures 6.8 and 6.9). Cambodia's debt distress rating improved in 2011 from a medium risk to a low risk, with the most recent joint IMF-World Bank Debt Sustainability Analysis indicating that its debt levels remain sustainable in the long run (IMF, 2013).

Cambodia's institutional and policy capacity, including debt management, have also improved, reflected by its upgrade to a medium performer based on the

Figure 6.8 External Public Debt *(In percent of GDP)*

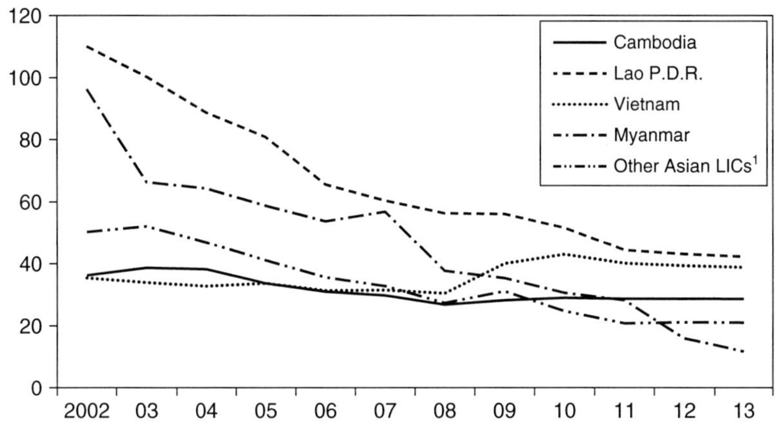

Sources: Country authorities; and IMF staff estimates and projections.
Note: LICs = low-income countries.
[1]Average of Bangladesh, Mongolia, and Nepal.

Figure 6.9 Public Debt and Debt Service

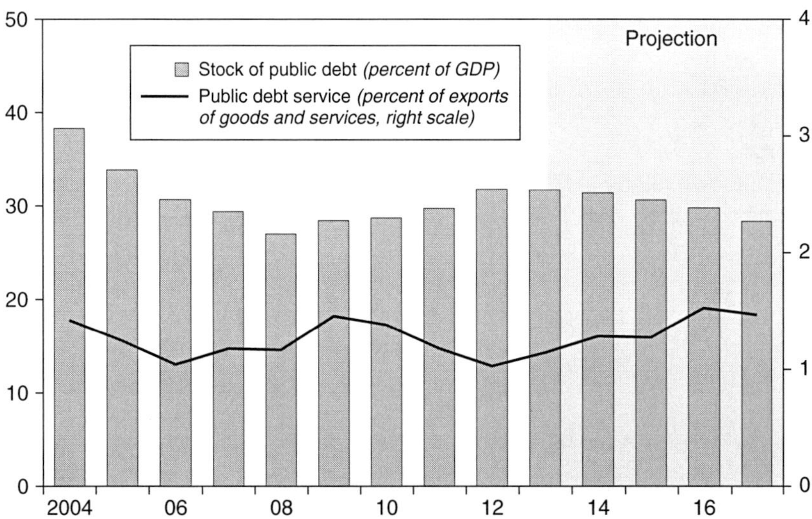

Sources: Cambodian authorities; and IMF staff estimates and projections.

World Bank's Country Policy and Institutional Assessment. However, risks could emerge from rapidly growing contingent liabilities related to power generation projects, as well as from government borrowing on less concessional terms. The government's power generation expansion plan envisages the completion of more than 30 projects under public-private partnerships by 2020, with a total investment cost outside the government's capital budget of about US$5½ billion (40 percent of 2012 GDP) over the intervening period.

The risks for the government by providing take-or-pay guarantees appear small in light of the need to resolve existing electricity shortages and the conservative demand forecasting scenarios underlying these projects. However, the sheer size of these projects and the difficulty in quantifying risks in advance for such complex infrastructure projects call for careful monitoring. If the risks and the potential contingent liabilities are not managed carefully, they could set back efforts at rebuilding fiscal space and jeopardize debt sustainability. As a result, fiscal space could be curtailed when it is most needed—that is, in the event of adverse economic shocks, when contingent liabilities are also more likely to be triggered.

Reforming Public Financial Management

Cambodia has made good progress in reforming public financial management, but various challenges remain (Box 6.2). The 2009 Public Expenditure and Financial Accountability assessment indicated that the credibility of the budget process has improved, with greater responsibility to program managers supported by enhanced internal controls and accountability mechanisms (Royal Government of Cambodia, 2010). The budget also provides a fair indication of the actual financial resources available, greater predictability of revenues, and good expenditure controls. The overall 2009 assessment score is broadly in line with the scores of other low-income countries in the region and reflects a strong performance, particularly in policy-based budgeting. However, progress in implementing the Financial Management Information System (FMIS) and in aligning government strategic goals, budget priorities, and donor support has been slower than expected. In addition, it will also be critical to integrate fiscal decentralization and public administration reforms with public financial management reforms.

Finally, establishing effective, accountable, and transparent governance will continue to be a major challenge (Figure 6.10). Progress has been made in developing effective governance after decades of conflict. However, various indicators, including the World Bank's governance indicators and Transparency International's corruption perception index, have revealed a strong persistence of weaknesses in governance. As discussed in Chapter 7, improving governance will play a critical role in mobilizing fiscal revenue.

POLICY PRIORITIES

In the near term, revenue mobilization is the most important reform to address fiscal challenges, and an integrated approach is needed to make the mobilization

BOX 6.2

Cambodia's Public Financial Management Reforms

The weaknesses in Cambodia's public financial management have deep roots. While shortcomings are common in many developing countries, Cambodia's devastating civil war and genocide destroyed human and institutional capacities for public financial management and led to a severe fragmentation of cash management. Years later, a subsequent boom of donor support overstretched the government's absorptive capacity and, as a result, many donor-funded projects remained outside the budget framework. In the early 2000s, Cambodia fell further behind comparable countries in its public financial management, particularly in the inadequacy of its budget formulation, its lack of credibility, its poor cash management, and the inappropriateness of its procurement framework. Cambodia launched the Public Financial Management Reform Program (PFMRP) in December 2004 and has made some progress since then. Implementation has focused on two platforms:

- **Platform One** reforms (2004–07) focused on strengthening revenue administration, streamlining the budget management process, consolidating government accounts, establishing an internal audit function, and improving budget implementation. Important progress was made in cash management and budget formulation. For example, the census of government bank deposit accounts was undertaken in 2007 in accordance with the implementation of the Treasury's Single Account roadmap; domestic payment arrears were cleared by end-2007; and the use of the banking system for revenue collection and expenditure payment increased substantially. Procurement rules and policies were also improved, with a reporting mechanism and post-review procedures introduced and a procurement manual issued. Finally, a better presentation of the capital budget, a midyear budget review, and laws on deconcentration and decentralization were introduced. However, progress in mobilizing revenue and improving expenditure composition remained limited.
- **Platform Two** reforms (2008–10) targeted the establishment of a new chart of accounts and budget classification, effective internal audit procedures, the introduction of a Financial Management Information System (FMIS), and the relocation of decision making and accountability to line ministries. Progress in these reforms has been slower than expected, leading to a call for reprioritization. The FMIS experienced significant delays owing to problems within the government as well as with ensuring adequate donor support. Few gains were made as well in a commensurate devolution of spending authority to line ministries. Progress in strengthening the charts of accounts and budget classification has been slower than expected.

On the positive side, reform gains under Platform One have continued to be consolidated, including the implementation of the budget law and improved cash management.

self-sustaining. Cambodia's revenue mobilization strategy should rely on a three-pronged approach: (i) improving revenue administration; (ii) implementing fair and efficient tax policies; and (iii) strengthening governance. The simultaneous implementation of reforms in these three areas is critical because progress in one area will create positive feedback to the others, making revenue mobilization more

Figure 6.10

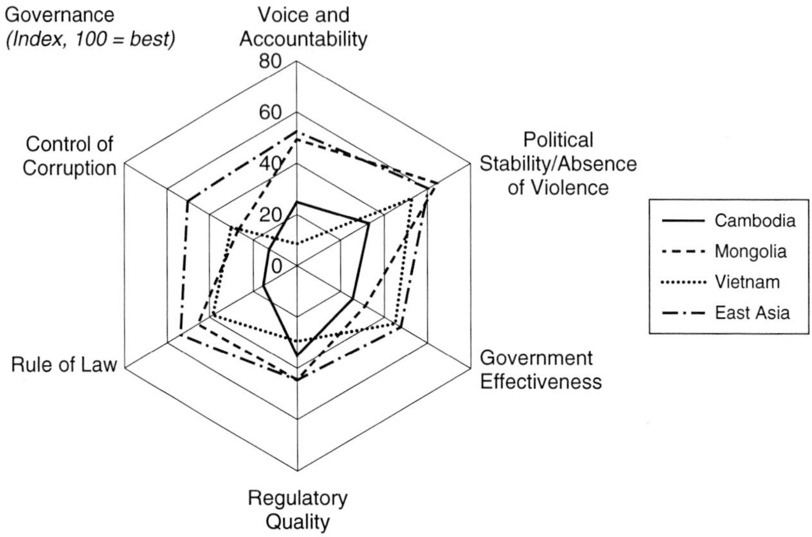

Source: World Bank Governnance Indicators (2011).

effective and self-sustaining. For example, better tax administration focusing on good taxpayer services and collecting tax arrears would make the tax system fairer and more efficient while at the same time improving compliance and reducing the incentives for corruption and evasion. Successful tax reforms in many developing countries have relied on an integrated approach, where strengthening revenue administration and reforming tax policy, supported by strong political will and technical capacity, play a critical role in enhancing revenue collection.

Cambodia's revenue mobilization strategy should prioritize policy actions that would generate substantial additional revenue, would create strong positive externalities, and could be implemented. These policy priorities include the following:

- *Revenue administration*: Collecting tax debts and improving the performance of the Large Taxpayer Department will raise additional revenue in the near term. Reprioritizing reform plans toward revenue-generating activities, establishing taxpayer services, developing human resources and information technology, and strengthening revenue forecasting will sustain revenue efforts going forward.
- *Tax policy:* Reforming the VAT and excise taxes will generate an immediate revenue impact. Continued tax policy reforms aimed at reducing exemptions and incentives, rationalizing corporate and personal income taxes, and implementing property taxes will help raise revenue over the medium term.
- *Governance:* Strengthening oversight and accountability of tax institutions and promoting transparency are critical to improve the performance and credibility of tax institutions.

Careful monitoring and management of fiscal contingent liabilities would safeguard fiscal space and help ensure debt sustainability. Cambodia adopted a new debt management strategy in 2012 aimed at managing debt risks, coordinating and implementing debt management policies, and developing debt management capacity. The strategy also emphasizes the importance of monitoring contingent liabilities, including those related to power generation and distribution projects. Under Cambodia's debt management strategy, continued efforts are needed to strengthen the evaluation, contracting, and monitoring of contingent liabilities, including the legal framework for public-private partnerships and the development of a new guarantee policy. It is also important to improve information sharing among government agencies regarding the size and status of contracts and embedded government guarantees. This could be done by setting up a central public-private partnership monitoring unit with "gateway powers" to evaluate and approve new partnership projects, enhancing fiscal transparency by adopting a ceiling on partnership guarantees, and listing all contingent liabilities and underlying guarantees in annual budget laws.

Stepping up efforts under the PFMRP will be critical to securing gains from enhanced revenue administration and to improve the effectiveness of priority spending. The efforts should include further strengthening the Platform One objectives, such as revenue mobilization, and at the same time moving toward achieving the goals under Platform Two (see Box 6.2). The priorities should be on those measures that are achievable in the near term and are of strategic importance, as follows:

- *Better recording and monitoring of donor-financed capital spending.* Budget execution and recording continue to be fragmented, especially with regard to donor-financed capital spending, hampering an assessment of fiscal and quasi-fiscal activities and effective budget planning. Better collaboration among donors is also needed to produce expenditure reports on a timely basis for donor-financed projects using the government charts or accounts. The inclusion of all off-budget donor-funded projects, such as technical assistance and NGO support, is also critical to improve transparency and accountability. All of these will help align donor support with government strategic priorities and improve budget formulation.
- *Continuing improvements in cash management, procurement, and audit.* This includes further strengthening government cash and bank account management, including cash flow forecasting and cash planning, as well as consolidating all government deposit accounts and using banks for transactions in all provinces. Enacting and implementing the new procurement law and moving toward the integration of the national public procurement systems under a single regulatory body would improve efficiency, transparency, and accountability. Strengthening the National Audit Authority and internal audit departments of agencies would improve both internal and external audits and help pave the way for the deconcentration process.
- *Designing and implementing a well-defined and integrated FMIS implementation action plan.* This would involve bringing together the three working

groups (line accountability, accounting standards, and budget execution) of the FMIS Steering Committee into a single plan that could be endorsed by development partners. The plan should also include a roadmap for a wider rollout of an FMIS that provides greater financial management and accountability for provincial and local administrations and line ministries. As a start, a further deepening of budget classifications at the line ministries is needed. All of these actions should be complemented by a comprehensive treasury support program to facilitate the implementation of the FMIS, and sustain and improve cash management as well as the movement toward the adaptation of international public sector accounting standards.

- *Ensuring that the PFMRP is aligned with and supported by two other public sector reforms, namely Public Administration Reform and Decentralization and Deconcentration Reform.* Reforming public administration is important because any delays in comprehensive civil service and institutional reforms could put further progress of PFRMP at risk. Continued progress in decentralization and in strengthening the capacity, governance, and transparency of public administration is also needed to implement the PFMRP in the provinces, districts, and municipalities.

Finally, without improvement in governance, the progress of fiscal reforms will be limited. Cambodia has put good governance at the core of its Rectangular Strategy Phase 2, under the National Strategic Development Plan. It envisages four major reform areas to strengthen governance: fighting corruption, legal and judicial reforms, public administration as well as decentralization and deconcentration reforms, and reforms of the armed forces (Royal Government of Cambodia, 2012). In line with the objectives of the National Strategic Development Plan, consistent implementation of governance reforms is critical to support reforms in other areas.

REFERENCES

International Monetary Fund, 2011, "Cambodia: 2010 Article IV Consultation," IMF Country Report No. 11/45 (Washington).

———, 2012, "Cambodia: 2011 Article IV Consultation," IMF Country Report No. 12/46 (Washington).

———, 2013, "Cambodia: 2012 Article IV Consultation," IMF Country Report No. 13/2 (Washington).

Royal Government of Cambodia, 2010, *Public Finance Management Assessment Cambodia*, Public Expenditure and Financial Accountability (PEFA) Report, available at www.pefa.org. (Washington: PEFA Secretariat).

———, 2012, *Mid-Term Review on the National Strategic Development Plan Update 2009–2013* (Phnom Penh).

World Bank, 2011, *Cambodia: More Efficient Government Spending for Strong and Inclusive Growth*, Integrated Fiduciary Assessment and Public Expenditure Review, World Bank Report No. 61694-KH (Washington: World Bank).

CHAPTER 7

Raising Funds for the Future: The Case for an Integrated Revenue Mobilization Strategy

TUBAGUS FERIDHANUSETYAWAN

This chapter proposes a strategy for mobilizing domestic revenue, which is the key to rebuilding the fiscal space, as discussed in Chapter 6. It draws on the findings of recent IMF technical assistance missions to Cambodia and prioritizes recommendations into a set of achievable and well-sequenced measures. The strategy is three-pronged: improving revenue administration, reforming tax policy, and strengthening governance. Simultaneous implementation in these three reform areas is critical, because good progress in one area would create positive feedback to the others, making revenue mobilization more effective and self-sustaining.

Cambodia has made progress in reforming tax policies and administration to raise fiscal revenue. A series of comprehensive tax reforms took place during the past two decades to modernize the tax system. Substantial reforms also took place in the area of revenue administration, anchored by the establishment of the Large Taxpayer Department (LTD) in the General Department of Taxation (GDT) and the introduction of an automated system for customs clearance. As a result, domestic revenue increased to more than 10 percent of GDP in 2008 from 6½ percent of GDP in 2003; it stayed broadly flat during 2009–11 before increasing again in 2012, for reasons noted in the previous chapter.

Despite this progress, revenue mobilization in Cambodia remains low by most standards, limiting fiscal space available to meet its myriad development needs. As discussed in Chapter 6, Cambodia's tax rates are competitive by regional standards, but revenue mobilization is constrained by excessive tax exemptions, low tax productivity, and weak collection. As a result, Cambodia's tax-to-GDP ratio, around 11 percent on average during 2010–12, remained low compared with the 24 percent average of Vietnam, the 15 percent average of Lao P.D.R., and the

---

This chapter is a shorter version of "Revenue Mobilization in Cambodia: Challenges and Policy Priorities," a background paper for the 2012 IMF Article IV Consultation with Cambodia, prepared by Tubagus Feridhanusetyawan (Asia and Pacific Department) in consultation with the IMF's Fiscal Affairs Department. It is based on a number of technical assistance reports prepared by IMF technical experts for the Cambodian authorities covering administrative reform issues, tax policy reforms and recommendations involving the tax regime for individual economic sectors.

18 percent average in other low-income countries in Asia (Bangladesh, Bhutan, Mongolia, and Nepal). The task of increasing government revenues will likely become more challenging over time, since the contribution of trade taxes is likely to decline as Cambodia implements its commitments under the ASEAN Free Trade Area (AFTA) and transitions to middle-income country status, with grant disbursements (currently at 3½ percent of GDP) likely to fall. Meanwhile, greater mobilization of fiscal revenues is imperative in the near term to rebuild government deposits if difficult and undesirable spending cuts are to be avoided, and also in the long term to maintain fiscal sustainability and meet Cambodia's vast development needs. In view of these challenges, the authorities have set an ambitious goal: to increase domestic revenue collection by ½ percent of GDP annually over the medium term.

In this chapter, we present a strategy to increase revenue collections over the medium term. We describe a comprehensive approach for mobilizing revenue and identifying specific policy priorities that can be implemented consistent with the findings of recent IMF technical assistance. We will distill and prioritize a long list of policy recommendations into a comprehensive set of achievable and well-sequenced measures. The first section will discuss the importance of pursuing a three-pronged strategy, with the other sections outlining specific policy priorities in each reform area.

A THREE-PRONGED STRATEGY

Cambodia's revenue mobilization strategy should rely on a three-pronged strategy: improving revenue administration, implementing fair and efficient tax policies, and strengthening governance (Figure 7.1). Simultaneous implementation of these three reform areas is critical, for two reasons.

First, progress in one area of reform would create positive dynamic feedback to the other two areas. For example, developing a fair, efficient, and simple tax system would make it easier for revenue administration agencies to collect taxes and promote good governance and transparency. Experience from other countries shows that simplifying the tax system would reduce the burden of administration, prevent tax ambiguity, and reduce incentives for corruption (see Box 7.1). Meanwhile, improving revenue administration, for example by establishing good taxpayer services and collecting tax arrears, would make the tax system fairer and more efficient while at the same time improving compliance. Similarly, strengthening governance by promoting accountability and transparency would help the revenue administration collect taxes and ensure the efficiency and fairness of the tax system.

The second reason simultaneous reform is critical is in the same vein: a lack of progress in one area will hamper reform efforts in another. For example, without a mechanism to strengthen oversight and transparency, it would be difficult to enforce rules and improve tax compliance. Similarly, if the tax regime is not implemented consistently owing to administrative weaknesses, it would be hard to analyze the framework and the performance of the tax system.

Figure 7.1 Cambodia: Three-Pronged Approach of Revenue Mobilization Strategy

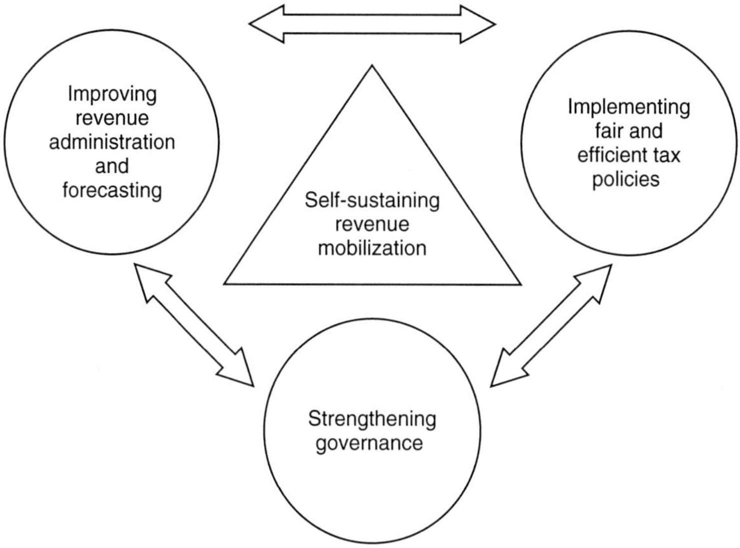

This three-pronged strategy is broadly in line with the lessons learned from successful tax reforms in many developing countries over the past two decades (Box 7.1; see IMF, 2011). Cross-country experience suggests that strengthened revenue administration, supported by strong political will and technical capacity, is critical to enhancing revenue mobilization. That said, estimating the revenue impact of administrative reforms alone could be difficult because the process is often complex, takes time, and involves other reforms. Past experiences also indicate the importance of simplifying tax laws, improving business processes, and segmenting the taxpayer population to better target administrative resources and improve compliance. However, challenges remain in strengthening human resources, improving coordination between domestic tax and customs administrations, reducing compliance costs, addressing noncompliance, and reducing corruption.

The priority should be on policy actions that would generate substantial additional revenue, create strong positive externalities, and be implemented without high cost. Cambodia has identified an extensive list of fiscal reforms, including policy actions to raise tax revenue. For example, the National Strategic Development Program and the Public Finance Management Reform Program have envisaged various measures to strengthen public financial management. Moreover, the IMF and other development partners have provided a long list of policy recommendations in recent years. However, policy actions need to be prioritized, sequenced, and implemented to make reforms more effective. The selection of measures should be based on their benefits (i.e., whether they are likely to generate additional revenue during the next three to five years), costs (i.e., practical implementation at the lowest cost possible), and strategic importance in supporting other reforms (i.e., creating positive externalities). Some measures are expected to

BOX 7.1

Cross-Country Experiences in Improving Revenue Mobilization

This box provides a few examples showing how countries have managed to increase revenue collection in a short period through comprehensive tax reforms supported by strong political will and technical assistance.

El Salvador implemented tax reforms by simplifying the tax regime and broadening the tax base during 2004–10. The reforms included restricting value added tax (VAT) zero-rating to exports; eliminating exemptions on interest earned in banks licensed abroad and on income from the interest and capital gains of individuals; establishing a tax on the registration of new vehicles; broadening the income tax withholding base for nonresidents; introducing a mixed (ad valorem and specific) system of excises on tobacco and alcoholic and other beverages, replacing the previous system of ad valorem rates to ensure that a reasonable tax is paid even on the least expensive products; introducing provisions to deal with transfer pricing, previously absent, and rules addressing thin capitalization; eliminating export subsidies; and increasing the tax on lottery prizes from 5 to 15 percent, partly to counter money laundering. These simplifications reduced the burden on tax administration and, as a result, tax revenue increased to 13.4 percent of GDP in 2010 from 10.9 percent of GDP in 2004.

Tanzania raised revenue collection without increasing tax rates by strengthening tax administration. The reform was guided by five-year plans of the semiautonomous Tanzania Revenue Authority and supported by development partners. Key reforms included introducing a common taxpayer identification number for all taxes; creating a large taxpayers department; consolidating VAT and income tax administration into the single, functionally structured Domestic Revenue Department; allocating geographical groups of taxpayers to specific teams with clear performance targets; and improving assistance to small taxpayers in understanding and complying with their obligations. A new income tax law (2004) introduced self-assessment and rationalized small taxpayer administration and an increase in the VAT threshold to focus on high-yield taxpayers. Policy reforms also simplified the personal income tax (PIT), including reducing the brackets and the top marginal rates, increasing the exempt amount under the PIT, and adjusting the presumptive income tax rates to reduce inconveniences to small-scale businesses. Customs reforms focused on interfacing operations with domestic revenue operations; better risk management; and introducing web-based customs clearance. These reforms helped raise tax collections to 15.3 percent of GDP in 2009 from 9 percent of GDP in 2000.

Vietnam implemented sweeping tax reforms by simplifying tax policies and strengthening tax administration guided by a five-year Tax Reform Plan (2005–10). The corporate income tax has been strengthened by unifying the rate structure, removing some incentives, permitting deductions, and transferring unincorporated businesses to the PIT. The VAT has been improved by restricting zero-rating to exports, eliminating the discrimination between domestic and imported products, and reducing exemptions. The PIT has also undergone comprehensive changes, such as introducing a tax on capital income, broadening the tax brackets, and lowering the top marginal rate. A new tax administration law was enacted in 2006 to combine all administrative procedures and broaden the powers of the General Department of Taxation (GDT) to administer the tax system. The GDT's headquarters and its network of tax offices were reorganized into functionally based units and connected by computer network, and a broad range of electronic applications were implemented. Steps have also been taken to upgrade staff skills; these actions have been supported by the creation of a tax college within the GDT. Reflecting these reforms, tax revenue averaged 23.7 percent of GDP during 2005–08, compared with 19.6 percent of GDP during 2001–04.

Source: IMF (2011).

TABLE 7.1

Cambodia: Policy Priorities for Revenue Mobilization

Reform area	Near-term priorities	Medium-term priorities
Revenue administration	Collecting tax debt and improving the performance of the Large Taxpayer Department.	Reprioritizing reform plans toward revenue-generating activities; establishing taxpayer services; developing human resources and information technology; strengthening revenue forecasting.
Tax policy	Reforming value added and excise taxes.	Focusing tax policy reforms on scaling back tax exemptions and incentives; limiting the estimated regime; rationalizing corporate and personal income taxes and property taxes.
Governance	Strengthening oversight and accountability and promoting transparency to improve the performance and credibility of tax institutions.	

Source: Various IMF technical assistance reports provided to the Cambodian authorities.

produce an immediate revenue impact, while others are included because they are expected to sustain revenue performance in the medium term (Table 7.1).

The remainder of this chapter will discuss specific policy priorities for each reform area to help focus and sequence reform implementation. It first focuses on revenue administration, which has lagged behind in reform progress but also has the largest potential to increase revenue in the near term. The discussion then turns to necessary reforms of tax policy and finally outlines some measures to strengthen governance.

IMPROVING REVENUE ADMINISTRATION AND FORECASTING

A stable and modern tax administration in Cambodia should be based on several key standards that guide revenue collecting agencies around the world. First, a proper legal framework is needed that provides an appropriate balance between the rights of taxpayers and the power of the tax agency, supported by efficient organizational and staffing arrangements. The framework should put in place a system of self-assessment, supported by streamlined collection systems and procedures, with the objectives of fostering voluntary taxpayer compliance, reducing compliance cost, and focusing enforcement efforts on taxpayers who pose a higher risk of evasion. Second, a service-oriented approach should be taken by the tax administration, whereby it operates as a trusted advisor and educator to help taxpayers meet their obligations voluntarily and is supported by risk-based audit and verification as well as dispute resolution mechanisms. Third, human resources management and information technology practices should be adopted: the former to provide incentives for high performance and ethical behavior of tax officials and the latter to promote the extensive use of a computerized system to help process taxpayer information effectively. Finally, a modern tax administration should have a mechanism to adopt ongoing institutional change for improvement, supported by an environment of integrity and good governance to ensure transparency and accountability. Although this chapter focuses on tax and customs revenue, improvements in nontax administration would also support revenue performance, albeit from a smaller base.

Near-Term Priorities

Cambodia faces a number of challenges in strengthening administration, which must be prioritized to maximize revenue collections (Table 7.2). The stock of tax debt including arrears is large, estimated at about half of the annual tax collection. At the same time, this figure is based on Cambodian tax officials' unilateral assessments, and lack of supporting evidence and accurate records on accumulated penalties and interest on old debt make the obligation difficult to collect. A task force should be set up to undertake forceful but professional collection activity against some of the worst offenders. For example, the task force could select some debts that are recent, significant, and uncontested, and secure the advance agreement from relevant senior officials to use appropriate collection measures for these cases.

The task force should maintain full records of all contacts with taxpayers and the actions taken and results, updated on a regular basis. Further efforts to strengthen the capacity of the LTD would also generate more revenue in the near term. The LTD contributes to more than three-fourths of revenue collection, but its performance has reached a plateau in recent years and further efforts are needed to enhance its capacity. For example, the LTD should be given full responsibility for all interactions with its taxpayer base, including oversight of the audit program. Improving the LTD's capacity to identify and address the major risks of noncompliance posed by its different types of taxpayers would help focus its limited resources on the least compliant taxpayers. In addition, since the service needs of large taxpayers are different from those of other taxpayers, the LTD needs to develop its own taxpayer service strategy. For instance, a range of tailored service initiatives, including improved relationship management for large taxpayers, could be established to develop respect and trust and encourage greater compliance.

In addition, rigorous audit activities are needed to support revenue collection. So far, audit activities have been fragmented, and efforts to investigate cases of

TABLE 7.2

Cambodia: Priorities for Improving Revenue Administration

Priority areas	Policy measures
Near term	
Debt collection: Start collecting large tax debts. Even a small proportion would generate significant additional revenue.	(1) Establish a task force to start addressing the most significant debt cases; (2) Develop protocols to delegate powers from relevant senior officials; (3) Develop tax installment payment arrangements; (4) Strengthen audit capacity.
Large Taxpayer Department (LTD): Strengthening the performance of LTD, which provides about 80 percent of tax collection, would raise overall revenue.	(1) Create a team within LTD to develop and maintain an understanding of every large taxpayer and risks; (2) Include the LTD arrears cases in the debt collection task force coverage; (3) Develop large taxpayer compliance strategy including service initiatives; (4) Relocate all large taxpayer risk assessment and audit functions to LTD.
Medium term	
Taxpayer services: A comprehensive strategy is needed to pull together the various elements of service delivery in order to improve taxpayers' compliance.	(1) Draw up action plans to ensure the implementation of the Department for Tax Services and Tax Arrears (DTSTA) operational work plan; (2) Continue seeking development partners to design and roll out a comprehensive taxpayer service strategy and allocate sufficient resources to taxpayer services functions. (3) Provide public information about avenues of appeal available to taxpayers.
Planning: Tax institutions have limited planning capacity and limited progress has been made in implementing action plans.	(1) Review the operational plans to prioritize activities and tasks, identify the resource needs, and set realistic targets. (2) Establish central reform office in tax institutions to implement and monitor reform programs.
Human resource development: Staff are skewed toward low-value activities, partly due to large number of small taxpayers and manual procedures. Meanwhile important functions like taxpayer services and debt collection are understaffed.	(1) Reorganize staff allocation by prioritizing revenue mobilization functions; (2) Allocate staff particularly at headquarters to strengthen governance, performance management, and monitoring; (2) Reform recruitment process to quickly fill vacancies.
Information technology (IT): The IT system is inadequate, procedures are predominantly manual and paper-based. Taxpayer information is unreliable and is not easily processed, consolidated, and shared, while the number of IT support staff is inadequate.	(1) Establish a business process and an IT reform program, including a dedicated full-time team and seek support from development partners. (2) Discuss funding option, including donor support, to develop IT infrastructure.
Revenue forecasting: Limited capacity of revenue analysis due to resource constraints and absence of automated systems and integrated database.	Strengthen revenue forecasting capacity at the Ministry of Economy and Finance (MEF) and all tax collecting agencies and improve coordination in setting and monitoring revenue targets.

Source: Various IMF technical assistance reports provided to the Cambodian authorities.

serious tax fraud have been limited, partly because of capacity constraints. In view of this, it would be a good start to assign all audit activities relating to taxpayers registered with the LTD to the department's staff. For other taxpayers, the Department of Enterprise Audit should have the full responsibility for designing and coordinating audit activity (including selection and audit guidelines) for all of the

GDT's audit teams (except those within the LTD). This would involve developing audit selection processes to better address noncompliance across the small- and medium-sized taxpayer segments and consolidating risk assessment activities in one central unit. It is also important to develop a standard audit manual which should cover routine audit procedures, and to design a system to record and transmit audit results to the appropriate departments, agencies, and units so that the risk assessment process, including information-sharing procedures, can be improved.

Medium-Term Priorities

Turning to medium-term priorities, the development of a comprehensive taxpayer service strategy would pave the way for sustained revenue collection. In Cambodia, basic taxpayer services are still lacking, such as providing taxpayers access to continuous tax education and written materials and alerting them to advisories, rulings, and dispute resolution processes. Therefore, a taxpayer services strategy is needed as a major component of the overall plan for improving taxpayers' compliance. This strategy, if formulated properly, would address what services could best assist taxpayers to comply with their obligations and how such services could be organized and delivered, including staffing and skill requirements. Sufficient resources for central and field-level taxpayer services would need to be reallocated to ensure successful delivery.

Concerning organization and planning, reorienting tax institutions' operations toward revenue-generating activities remains the top priority. With no organizational separation between tax policy and tax administration, the work on policy and legal issues has often drawn valuable resources away from revenue-generating activities. The work on legal initiatives should also be focused on areas that will improve revenue yield, such as reducing the "gray" areas to improve tax compliance. The GDT Strategic Plan 2011–14 is a good starting point, but more prioritization is needed, particularly in aligning the planned activities with the overall strategic direction and resource availability. For example, taxpayer services feature prominently in the technical assistance supported by development partners, but it has not received full recognition as a strategic priority. Therefore, the tax institutions need to reorient themselves toward the identified priorities for generating and sustaining revenue collection, such as improving taxpayer services, where limited resources are currently deployed.

Efforts to strengthen human capital should focus on reallocating staff toward high-value activities that generate revenue. The limited number of skilled and experienced staff is currently skewed toward low-value activities, partly because of the structure of the tax system (large numbers of small taxpayers) and procedures, which are predominantly manual. The most qualified staff are also stretched by numerous tasks, such as participating in ad hoc policy teams, leaving limited resources for operational work. Meanwhile, functions that ought to have a higher strategic value, such as taxpayer services and debt collection, have been understaffed. More staff are needed to work on governance, performance management, and monitoring roles to strengthen oversight of tax institution performance. Finally, a program to strengthen human capital should be supported by improvements in the recruitment process to quickly bring in new staff once a vacancy arises.

The information technology (IT) systems are currently inadequate. Developing effective and efficient IT systems may take time, but it is critical to sustain revenue mobilization over the medium term. At present, procedures are predominantly manual and paper-based and taxpayer information is not easily processed, shared, or consolidated. The lack of IT systems also contributes to face-to-face tax assessments that create opportunities for corruption. Without substantial improvement in the IT systems, progress in improving core tax administration procedures (taxpayer registration and services, returns filing, revenue collection, and arrears management) will be limited. However, significant investment is required to obtain and implement a good IT system as well as the resources to manage and sustain the system. Therefore, the priorities should be on developing and implementing an IT reform agenda within the overall reform program, and establishing a dedicated, full-time team charged with improving business processes and IT systems. Further support from development partners will be needed to advance these efforts and maintain full transparency and accountability in developing the IT systems.

Along with the development of these systems, the management of tax registration should continue to be improved. Taxpayer registration has not kept up with business development nationwide, evidenced by the fact that the number of registered business taxpayers is much smaller than the number of registered business establishments. At a minimum, the ongoing process of cleansing the existing registration databases should proceed together with centralizing national registration responsibilities under the Department of Taxpayer Services and Tax Arrears. Meanwhile, the authorities should develop a plan to broadly expand the taxpayer base, with appropriate resources and development partner support, aimed at creating a single, automated, registration database for all taxpayers. Expanding the number of registered taxpayers requires improving control systems to be able to handle new registrants effectively.

Revenue forecasting needs to be strengthened to help establish appropriate revenue targets in annual budgets and medium-term frameworks. The capacity for forecasting revenue remains limited owing to human resource constraints and the absence of integrated and automated systems to capture and process data. For example, various performance statistics, including audit results and arrears stocks, are held by each department and by the tax branches, but they are not consolidated centrally on a regular basis. The Ministry of Economy and Finance recently started a program to enhance the revenue forecasting capacity of its Fiscal Policy Department, supported by technical assistance from the IMF. This important initiative should include establishing effective coordination between the ministry, GDT, and the General Department of Customs and Excise to improve revenue analysis, set revenue targets, and monitor performance.

Good progress has been made in customs revenue collection, and the challenge is to sustain strong performance going forward. The collection of customs duties, export taxes, import VAT, and other trade taxes has been improved since 2009 by implementing reforms in customs procedures and techniques, including the implementation of the Automated System for Customs Data. Despite this progress, more efforts are needed to strengthen the customs intelligence and antismuggling functions, both at headquarters and in provincial branches, to detect fraud and reduce smuggling. Steps should also be taken to continue strengthening capacity in import valuation and post clearance audits.

In addition, reform priorities should include preparing the development of the Cambodia National Single Window (i.e., processing trade documents at a single location or agency) and the implementation of the regional priority "Asia cargo highway" (i.e., trade facilitation initiatives to create seamless flows of goods) by 2015. Improving customs administration would also be critical in offsetting the potential customs revenue losses from the implementation of AFTA.

IMPLEMENTING EFFICIENT AND FAIR TAX POLICIES

Cambodia could improve its tax regimes by following standard principles of *efficiency, equity,* and *simplicity* (IMF, 2010). The efficiency principle means that taxes should interfere as little as possible with relative prices and resource allocations, creating minimal distortion in the economy. The equity principle ensures that taxpayers under a similar situation should pay similar taxes and that the individual tax burden should reflect the ability to pay. The simplicity or ease-of-implementation principle means that taxes should be designed to minimize taxpayers' cost of compliance and tax institutions' cost of administering taxation. Based on these principles as well as cross-country experiences, reforming indirect taxation, such as the VAT and excise taxes, would generate a more immediate impact on revenue collection. Meanwhile, reforming direct taxation, such as profit and income taxes, will also be critical to sustain tax collection in the long run. The priorities for tax policy reforms are presented in Table 7.3.

Cambodia has two tax regimes for business taxpayers: the real regime and the estimated regime. The real regime centers on the VAT and the standard income tax and is focused on larger taxpayers, while the estimated regime is anchored by a 2 percent turnover tax and a profits tax, mainly to bring smaller taxpayers into the system. Tax collected from the estimated regime is very small, but the number of estimated taxpayers is large in comparison to those subject to the real regime, with current estimates placing them at more than 40,000. Despite this, low compliance and weak enforcement have contributed to poor revenue collections from this group. Little information exists on taxpayers in the estimated tax regime, since they are monitored mainly by the district offices and are not registered and assigned tax ID numbers, which creates opportunities for tax evasion.

Near-Term Priorities

As a first priority, tax policy reforms should focus on unifying the VAT thresholds for all taxpayers and registering all taxpayers, including in the estimated regime, with tax ID numbers. The VAT is the largest single source of tax revenue in Cambodia, but tax productivity remains low owing to a narrow tax base and weak enforcement. At present, VAT taxpayers are primarily large taxpayers, contributing about 90 percent of the domestic VAT. However, several VAT thresholds exist

TABLE 7.3

Cambodia: Priorities for Strengthening Tax Policy

Priority areas	Policy measures
Near term	
Value added tax (VAT): Revenue productivity is low due to narrow tax base, weak enforcement, and little information on taxpayers of the estimated regime because they are not registered.	(1) Apply one threshold to all types of taxpayers; (2) Make registration with tax ID mandatory for all taxpayers; (3) Eliminate exemptions for electricity; (4) Adopt partial exemptions system for financial institutions by establishing rules to define the different kinds of financial services.
Excise tax: Low collection due to small amount of tax on standard excisable products. Restructuring the excise system would generate immediate revenue impact.	(1) Rationalize the list of imported goods taxed; (2) Increase the number of petroleum products taxed; (3) Consolidate the ad valorem and additional taxes on fuels into one specific, indexed, tax; (4) Increase excise tax and customs duty on diesel to equal the rates on gasoline; (5) Tax tobacco with specific, indexed, excise tax.
Medium term	
Tax incentives: Profit tax collections are low partly owing to various tax incentives that are unnecessary as Cambodia's tax rate is low and competitive.	(1) Limit tax holidays to specific industries for certain periods with no extensions; (2) Phase out tax holidays, grandfathering existing investors for specified time period.
Estimated tax regime: The process is labor intensive and the collection is low. The presumptive tax is determined by the GDT after verification, consultation, and negotiation with taxpayers.	(1) Replace the negotiation system with simple, transparent, and consistent procedures for determining profits to improve governance and transparency.
Personal income tax: The collection is low due to narrow base, low compliance, and weak enforcement.	(1) Address low compliance through strong enforcement. (2) Refrain from changing tax policies without any efforts in strengthening administration; (3) Streamline the PIT from five to three rates (for example, 0, 10, and 20 percent) and reduce deductions.
Capital income tax: Highly uneven statutory rates on different sources of capital income and no tax on capital gains.	(1) Tax interest income with a standard rate of 15 percent. (2) Introduce uniform taxation on individual capital income consistent with the principle of dual income tax. (3) Prepare the introduction of a capital gains tax.
Property tax: The introduction of property taxation in urban areas is a positive step, and consistent and transparent implementation of property taxation across the country would provide additional source of revenue.	(1) Review the implementation of property taxation to ensure it works effectively before expanding it across the country. (2) Strengthen property valuation procedures, including reassessment every five years and provide independent dispute resolution.

Source: Various IMF technical assistance reports provided to the Cambodian authorities.

depending on the type of businesses, and this increases collection costs and creates opportunities for tax evasion. The highest threshold (US$125,000 a year for businesses providing goods) is relatively high compared with the threshold commonly applied in countries in the region (US$50,000), while the lowest threshold (US$31,250 for unincorporated government contractors) is too low. Unifying the thresholds to the level comparable to the regional average would simplify the tax regime and increase revenue substantially.

The system of negotiation in determining tax in the estimated regime should be removed. The estimated regime is essentially a presumptive tax, and the amount of tax is determined by tax officials after verification and consultation with the taxpayer. This system of negotiation is resource-intensive and open to abuse, leading to potential revenue leakage. Removing the system of negotiation would improve transparency and help taxpayers meet their tax obligations. For example, the regulations could be modified to clearly define the profit margins with simple rules, which could be made publicly available and applied consistently to all taxpayers. The simplified profit margins would also make the tax system simpler and more transparent, reduce opportunities for abuse, and free up GDT resources that could be focused on more revenue-generating tasks. It is also important to undertake a comprehensive study of the taxpayer population under the estimated tax regime, using the results of the economic census, to gauge the revenue potential of these taxpayers. Formulating new strategies for bringing more of them into the tax net, for example by strengthening enforcement and audit activities, would raise revenue collection.

Restructuring the current excise system could have an immediate revenue impact. Although Cambodia levies excise taxes on services such as telecommunications, hotel accommodations, and motor vehicles, its revenue collection is low mainly owing to the small amount of tax on standard excisable products such as tobacco, carbonated and alcoholic beverages, and diesel fuel. In almost all of these categories, the tax rates in Cambodia are about one-half to one-third the rates in neighboring countries. As a start, the reference prices used to calculate taxes and the ad valorem tax rates could be raised and, at a later stage, these ad valorem taxes could be replaced by specific taxes with indexation. Rationalizing the list of imported goods subject to tax would also ensure that all standard goods, including all petroleum products such as liquefied petroleum gas and kerosene, are properly taxed. In addition, raising the excise tax on diesel to the rate applied to gasoline and eliminating the differential taxation of domestic and imported tobacco products could raise revenue in the near term.

Medium-Term Priorities

Another priority is to scale back tax incentives, including income tax holidays and exemptions on the VAT, import duties, and excise taxes. Tax incentives involve a loss of current and future revenue and create different tax treatments between and within sectors, leading to distorted resource allocation. Moreover, they create opportunities for tax abuse and corruption and tend to attract footloose firms that leave as soon as the incentive expires. In fact, taxes are not the only important factor in investment decisions, and the benefits of tax incentives may be reversed if a foreign investor is from a country that taxes its residents on a worldwide basis. There are also other concerns specific to Cambodia that need to be addressed, mainly a lack of effective monitoring to prevent abuse and revenue leakage; uncertainty for both taxpayers and administrators about the treatment of companies with multiple Qualified Investment Projects; and a lack of cost and benefit analyses of the incentives.

By and large, tax incentives in Cambodia are unnecessary given the country's competitive tax regime. As discussed in Chapter 6, the VAT rate is 10 percent; the corporate tax rate is 20 percent; and the highest PIT rate is 20 percent—each lower than the typical rates for other low-income countries in the region. Therefore, tax holidays should be phased out in the medium term to prevent more revenue losses. If incentives are to be granted for investment, then accelerated depreciation or investment tax credits should be provided. If tax incentives are to be provided in Special Economic Zones, they should not include income tax incentives, but be restricted to import duties and VAT on exports with close monitoring. However, removing these incentives and their harmful effects may be politically challenging in the near term. Therefore, during the transition period, tax holidays could be limited by applying them to a few specific sectors with clear criteria and for a period of no more than three years with no extensions (grandfathering existing investors for the remaining period of their time-bound incentives). The granting of tax incentives should rest with one agency, such as the Council for the Development of Cambodia, and the laws granting them should be consolidated into one law, preferably the Law on Taxation, and with sunset clauses adopted in all other laws containing tax incentives.

Personal income taxation. Broadening the PIT base through stronger enforcement has large revenue potential. The PIT base is currently very narrow, with only an estimated 1½ percent of the urban employed liable. Reduction in the threshold for zero tax rates may generate more collections, although the cause of low revenue is likely weak enforcement. Therefore, changes in tax policy should not be made without other reforms aimed at improving revenue administration, including strengthening enforcement through a salary withholding tax.

Capital income taxation. Continued reforms in streamlining capital income taxation would sustain revenue collection over the medium term. Currently, Cambodia's capital tax has highly uneven statutory rates on the different sources of capital income received by individuals. For example, interest income is taxed at final withholding rates of 4, 6, or 15 percent, depending on whether the interest is paid by banks or by nonbanks. The large variation in the taxation of personal capital income has a number of undesirable effects. First, the disparity in effective tax rates has efficiency costs by distorting portfolio choices of individuals. Second, it opens up loopholes by inviting tax arbitrage by providing incentives to invest in assets that generate lightly taxed or nontaxable returns, such as capital gains. Finally, current policies for taxing capital income violate equity considerations by allowing lower effective rates on income accruing mainly to the better-off segments of the population.

To address these issues, over the medium term Cambodia should adopt the principles of the dual income tax to prevent tax arbitrage, taxing all interest income and other capital income, such as dividends, at a low uniform rate of 10–15 percent. In the longer run, a capital gains tax should be introduced as an integral part of the PIT.

Property taxation. The introduction of property taxation in the urban areas in 2011 was a positive step and should help pave the way for countrywide implementation over the medium term. However, a review of its implementation needs to be done to ensure that it is working effectively before expanding it across the country. Based on existing reviews, the law could be strengthened by requiring property valuations to be reassessed at least every five years and by indexing property values—for example, to the consumer price index—in the interim. In addition, ensuring clear procedures for valuation and providing an independent dispute resolution process are important. In the longer term, the tax rate could be increased to at least 0.5 percent of the assessed property value, providing that local authorities, who are responsible for assessing, collecting, and enforcing the tax, have some discretion to set rates within a small range determined by the central government. At the same time, consideration could be given to repealing the tax on unused land and reducing the rate of the property transfer tax, which may discourage investment.

Resource-based taxation. Although Cambodia does not rely on resource-based revenue, formulating a resource-based tax regime is important to ensure that Cambodia gets the most benefit from the extraction of its mining, petroleum, gas, and other natural resources. Because of the specific characteristics of resource projects, the resource-based taxation regime is generally separated from the general taxation regime. For example, an exploration project could be lengthy and risky, the amount of capital to develop a mine could be lumpy, and capital could be captive and not transportable. In addition, revenues and costs can be volatile, driven by mineral and fuel prices, and it takes time to recoup a large upfront investment. Therefore, an appropriate resource-based tax regime should strike a balance between maximizing tax collection from the rents and providing an incentive for companies to invest in mining activities. The instruments of the mining regime include direct taxes, such as the corporate income tax and the profit tax, and indirect taxes, such as royalties, export duties, and import duties. Other nontax instruments can also be used, such as production-sharing arrangements and state equity participation.

Before a resource-based fiscal regime is established, Cambodia should follow a cautious approach in signing agreements on resource extraction projects that include tax and nontax provisions. While agreements on prospecting licenses for exploration could be granted based on the current mineral laws, agreement on mining leases for extraction should be prepared carefully to ensure that Cambodia gets the most benefits. Mining and petroleum agreements are complex and often difficult to implement and oversee. These agreements determine how profits are divided between the government and investors and how their costs are to be paid or recovered. In view of these factors, the government should consider hiring truly independent experts to help formulate and evaluate the contracts. In addition, contracts and regulatory matters should be disclosed publicly, including by participating in the Extractive Industries Transparency Initiative, to promote transparency in the process and the accountability of public officials.[1]

[1]The EITI is a global standard that promotes revenue transparency and accountability in the extractive sector by monitoring and reconciling company payments and government revenues from oil, gas, and mining at the country level (see www.eiti.org).

International taxation. Finally, Cambodia needs to strengthen its international taxation regime as its economy develops and becomes more internationally integrated. The provisions on international taxation are currently limited. For example, Cambodia has no double tax agreements (DTAs), which play an important role in determining the taxation rights of a country in which income is sourced. However, because reforming international taxation may take time and require substantial capacity building in formulating and implementing complex taxation regimes, it should be viewed as a medium-term priority. Nonetheless, the ongoing efforts to formulate DTAs with countries that are close trading partners or are significant sources of foreign direct investment should continue. In the process, the interaction between DTAs and tax incentives should not be overlooked, because these incentives, as currently structured in Cambodia, render the benefits of DTAs virtually ineffective. A foreign country would have less incentive to consider signing a treaty on DTAs with Cambodia if its own companies were not subject to tax in Cambodia because of the incentives. In addition, developing transfer pricing rules and improving the capacity to administer them would help strengthen Cambodia's international tax regime.

STRENGTHENING GOVERNANCE

Effective revenue mobilization requires strong political commitment supported by accountable and transparent institutions. Political commitment is essential for successful reforms. Lasting reforms require deep institutional change across all dimensions—policies, procedures, systems, human resources, and organizational behavior. Strong accountability and transparency—both internally (management) and externally (governance and oversight)—would improve the performance and increase the credibility of tax institutions, thereby raising the public's perception of and confidence in the tax system. In this context, Cambodia's priorities for improving governance are presented in Table 7.4.

Strengthening the oversight and accountability of tax institutions is the key to improving governance. The GDT and GDCE are responsible to the Ministry of Economy and Finance and are required to obtain its approval for a wide range of

TABLE 7.4

Cambodia: Priorities for Strengthening Governance

Priority areas	Policy measures
Oversight: Limited oversight of the General Department of Taxation's (GDT) and General Department of Customs and Excise's (GDCE) operations and performance. **Transparency:** Officials have considerable discretion in the application of tax laws due to weaknesses of management systems, process, and controls, and limited information and assistance to taxpayers.	Create the political will to strengthen oversight and accountability of GDT and GDCE, and within the GDT and GDCE. (1) Create systematic programs for taxpayer education, advice, and interpretation of the laws; (2) Remove the complex system of tax negotiation and abolish informal taxpayer-facing activities; (3) Strengthen management and supervisory controls.

Source: Various IMF technical assistance reports provided to the Cambodian authorities.

actions, but the ministry's oversight of these departments' overall operations and performance remains a challenge. Meanwhile, within tax institutions, the headquarters' oversight of organizational performance and individual tax officials is also limited, partly because of capacity constraints and system weaknesses. This hinders effective enforcement and opens the door for rent-seeking behavior. Therefore, strong oversight and accountability are needed, which could be provided by the Ministry of Economy and Finance directly or by an independent governance board, as is the case in many other countries. Strengthening oversight and accountability should be the core of governance reform, drawing from inside and outside the government, including from the private sector.

Cambodia has much scope to improve transparency in tax policies and administration. For example, the provision of information, assistance, and advice to taxpayers is generally limited. There are no systematic programs to inform taxpayers about their rights and obligations and enable them to obtain greater certainty in managing and paying their taxes. The dispute resolution process contained in the law has not been implemented effectively, and current processes are inadequate. At the same time, and partly as a result of weak oversight, officials have considerable discretion in the application of procedures. This discretion creates a high risk of informality, particularly in taxpayer-tax official interactions, and threatens the integrity of the tax system and the reputation of tax institutions.

In view of these shortcomings, continued efforts to improve transparency will play a critical role in strengthening tax institutions' governance. Creating systematic programs for taxpayer education, advice, and interpretation of the laws would be a good start to improve taxpayers' confidence and perception. Removing the complex system of tax negotiation, particularly in the estimated tax regime, and abolishing informal taxpayer-tax official interactions would go a long way toward improving taxpayers' confidence in an even-handed and fair system. Automation and stronger management controls and oversight are crucial for this. Establishing processes for independent reviews of GDT and GDCE decisions and for dispute resolutions would also boost transparency. Finally, better governance of tax institutions would help enhance the progress made so far in reforming tax policies and administration.

REFERENCES

International Monetary Fund (IMF), 2010, "From Stimulus to Consolidation: Revenue and Expenditure Policies in Advanced and Emerging Economies," IMF Policy Paper (Washington).

———, 2011, "Revenue Mobilization in Developing Countries," IMF Policy Paper (Washington).

CHAPTER 8

Can the Riel Prosper? Welding Financial Development and Dedollarization

PHURICHAI RUNGCHAROENKITKUL

Cambodia has one of the most dollarized economies in the world. While dollarization has played some part in anchoring the country's macroeconomic stability and sustaining economic growth over the last two decades, whether it provides the right framework is highly contentious.

This chapter discusses how Cambodia's dedollarization objective is interlaced with the goals of developing its financial sector and, ultimately, pursuing greater monetary policy effectiveness. It argues that a carefully designed and sequenced introduction of financial and market development initiatives, accompanied by regulatory measures and clear communication about the policy path, could minimize any unintended setback on dedollarization and enable the country to achieve its dual objective.

Apart from the fact that dollarization was not Cambodia's official choice to begin with, the costs to the country associated with it are high, as shown in Chapter 3. First, the loss of seigniorage revenue alone is likely to be non-negligible.[1] Second, the lack of monetary independence limits the authorities' ability to respond to shocks, a particularly costly constraint considering the economy's rapid integration with the region and the world and the increasingly volatile global capital movements. Third, the fact that banking sector balance sheets are largely denominated in dollars also limits the authorities' role as a lender of last resort in addressing financial stability risks. Moreover, Cambodia has come a long way in rebuilding an economic and financial infrastructure capable of maintaining macroeconomic stability in the context of independent monetary policy.

As a result, a longstanding ambition, shared by both the government and the central bank, has been to dedollarize the economy.[2] At the same time, with the economy growing rapidly, the demand for efficient financial services and further

[1]Cited as "a main cost of high dollarization in Cambodia," de Zamaróczy and Sa (2002) calculated that, as of 2001, lost seigniorage revenue in Cambodia ranged between 0.7 percent and 1.5 percent of GDP.
[2]The government has stated that "Promotion of the riel has been adopted as government policy over the short to medium term, and dedollarization as the long-term goal" (Royal Government of Cambodia (2012, p.9).

financial development is also building. Moreover, monetary policy cannot be effective without a developed financial market that helps transmit the policy actions to economywide monetary conditions. With the balance sheets of Cambodian banks being almost entirely in U.S. dollars, making further progress in financial development is easiest done by promoting dollar-based financial activity, a seeming conflict with the dedollarization objective.

Against this background, we start from the basic premise that the critical ingredients for a successful transition toward an independent and market-based monetary policy framework consist of both making significant progress in dedollarization and developing financial markets to create an effective monetary transmission mechanism. In order to reconcile the dual objectives of dedollarization and financial development, the chapter discusses strategic options and their relative merits and highlights the importance of a clear communication strategy to support them.

TOWARD GREATER MONETARY POLICY EFFECTIVENESS

Dollarization in Cambodia occurs both in terms of *currency substitution* and *asset substitution*. Under the former, the U.S. dollar widely serves the dual functions as a medium of exchange and as a unit of account in everyday transactions by households and businesses.[3] At the same time, with foreign currency deposits accounting for more than 90 percent of total deposits, there is also an extensive dollarization in the interest-bearing assets. This *asset substitution* on the part of households leaves banks with dollar-dominated liabilities, which are perpetuated when they extend loans mostly in dollars to hedge against currency risks. Both sides of banks' balance sheets are therefore denominated largely in dollars, which have become an accepted medium of exchange among banks. The literature sometimes refers to the phenomenon as *financial dollarization*. The current structure of dollarization in Cambodia is summarized schematically in Figure 8.1.

Different aspects of dollarization help reinforce each other. Widespread currency substitution at the level of firms and households makes it easier for asset substitution and financial dollarization to flourish, and vice versa. Because of this multifaceted and interdependent nature of Cambodia's dollarization, the strategy for pursuing monetary independence cannot be approached separately through financial market development. For example, while developing an interbank market in U.S. dollars would help promote financial development, it carries a risk

[3]Using a portfolio balance approach, Ize and Yeyati (2003) show that the degree of currency substitution is an increasing function of inflation volatility, but a decreasing function of exchange rate volatility. However, because in Cambodia's case the dollar also serves as a unit of account and households' local consumption basket is to a significant degree denominated in dollars, the basic portfolio view need not hold. Instead, in this context, the degree of dollarization should increase with the expected depreciation of the local currency, as the latter would lower the purchasing power of the riel-denominated portfolio.

Figure 8.1 Different Guises of Dollarization

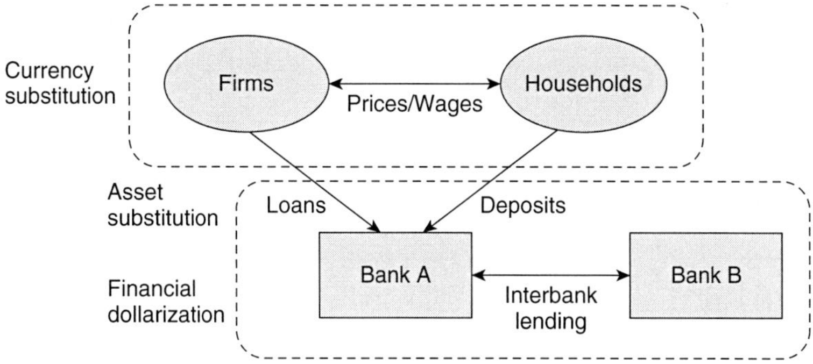

of further entrenching financial dollarization and consequently currency substitution. Whether such an initiative would constitute a step forward in the quest for an independent monetary policy framework is therefore unclear.

Meanwhile, financial development is both an integral part of broader economic development and a necessary foundation for effective monetary policy transmission. Without financial development, an independent monetary policy and financial intermediation in general would be ineffective. Short of a significant reduction in dollarization, financial development would do little to enhance monetary independence (and possibly quite the opposite). Therefore, to achieve the ultimate goal of effective and independent monetary policy, Cambodia needs to make progress in both dedollarization and financial development.

A body of cross-country evidence has highlighted the roles of macroeconomic stability, good governance, and institutional quality in helping economies dedollarize (see De Nicolo, Honohan, and Ize, 2003; Yeyati, 2005; and Asel, 2010; for example), but few studies have looked at the relationship between the two objectives of dedollarization and financial development. Country-specific anecdotes, however, confirm potential linkages between the two. For example, the development of a local currency government bond market has been identified as a contributing factor to the successful dedollarization in Peru (Garcia-Escribano, 2010).

While macroeconomic stability is a necessary condition for successful dedollarization, it is not sufficient. With the second objective of financial development, it becomes even clearer that macroeconomic stability must be augmented by other initiatives that are tailored to Cambodia's circumstances. We propose in this chapter that the strategy to weld dedollarization to financial development be guided by the following general considerations:

- The strategy should spell out in advance the *sequencing* of initiatives that together make up a credible plan for dedollarization as well as a commitment to making steady progress in laying the foundation for an independent monetary policy framework.

- The dedollarization strategy should be *credible* and *comprehensive* and aim to address all aspects, including currency substitution, asset substitution, and financial dedollarization.
- Financial development initiatives should proceed but, wherever possible, *avoid perpetuating* the degree of asset substitution and financial dollarization. When financial development and dedollarization come into conflict, measures should be introduced to lessen the tension between the two objectives.

FINANCIAL DEVELOPMENT INITIATIVES

What are the potential frictions between dedollarization and financial development? In Cambodia's case, the creation of an interbank market and of a stock exchange with its potential spillovers to the nascent foreign exchange market are the most relevant examples of how financial development initiatives impact progress toward dedollarization. This section reviews both development initiatives in detail and discusses their relationship to dedollarization.

Interbank Market

A new initiative is the development of a collateralized interbank market. Currently, qualified commercial banks have access to a fixed-rate deposit facility at the National Bank of Cambodia (NBC). While the facility is available in both riels and dollars, the extent of financial dollarization means that these deposits are almost entirely denominated in U.S. dollars. The initiative aims to collateralize them by introducing negotiable certificates of deposit (NCDs), which can be traded and used as collateral for interbank lending through repurchase agreements. It is hoped that collateralization will help alleviate counterparty risks, reduce banks' precautionary motives for maintaining excessive liquidity, and promote an efficient interbank market and commercial banking activities. Ultimately, a fully developed interbank market could serve as the platform for implementing open market operations.

Specific features of NCDs constitute a critical step of the strategic plan. As discussed above, the choice of currency denomination, for both pricing and settlement, is particularly relevant for the tension between financial market development and dedollarization goals. A closely related issue is whether the NBC should securitize the deposits outright or issue entirely new securities and gradually phase out the existing fixed deposit facility. Under the first approach, the NBC would effectively have to denominate the securities in U.S. dollars by default, since nearly all current deposits are in U.S. dollars. Under the second approach, the NBC could issue new securities in riels as well as in U.S. dollars, but the demand for riel-denominated securities is likely to be very low in the near term given Cambodia's high degree of dollarization.

Regardless of currency denomination, the NBC must also ensure that the new securities will be preferred by banks to the currently available fixed deposits, for example by announcing a timetable for phasing out the fixed deposits. Although the NCDs may command a collateral premium or pay higher coupons relative to fixed deposit rates, the market prices of these tradable securities could adjust to reflect their inherent values. In any case, the two distinct liquidity management instruments remain imperfect substitutes owing to their different short-term volatilities. Fixed deposits provide deterministic cash flows, paying a fixed rate of interest at maturity but incurring a penalty for premature withdrawals, which could give rise to a "kinked" payoff. On the other hand, NCDs would likely provide a smoother payoff profile than fixed deposits, but are subject to market risks.

These nuances mean that (i) the two instruments may attract demand from different types of holders, creating a form of market segmentation, and (ii) the relative demand may depend on prevailing market conditions. For banks with more frequent liquidity needs and higher market-risk tolerance, the NCDs offer greater benefits compared to fixed deposits owing to their collateral value and smoother payoffs. For others, the market risks associated with the NCDs are more binding, making them less attractive. Similarly, during periods of high market volatility and/or low trading liquidity, the fixed deposit facility may become more attractive.

Capital and Foreign Exchange Markets

The effect of market design on financial dollarization is also evident in the case of the Cambodia Securities Exchange, which began trading its first and only stock in April 2012. The stock market was designed to allow transactions to be settled in both dollars and riels, although the listing is required to be in the local currency only. Available information suggests that all trading activity of the debut issue (stock of the Phnom Penh Water Supply Authority) so far has been settled exclusively in riels. A combination of factors may have contributed to this outcome. First, given the riel quotation, any settlement in a foreign currency necessitates a second agreement in the exchange rate, adding to the complexity and risk of the trade. Second, if no exchange rate is agreed among the counterparties within two days of the transaction, the settlement is in riels, as dictated by regulation. That the listing requirement in local currency can effectively encourage greater use of the riel in settlement should serve as an important lesson.

Developing a wholesale foreign exchange market will also become more pressing as the economy makes further progress in financial dedollarization and in developing financial markets, given the attendant growth in and demand for, and the supply of, riels. As recommended by the IMF during the 2012 Article IV consultation, the NBC should scale down its direct involvement in the foreign exchange market, organize a wholesale market with large commercial banks at the core, and allow the market to clear itself. With that market infrastructure in place, wholesale foreign exchange activity should grow in line with the gradual progress in financial dedollarization. When the market becomes sufficiently deep and liquid, the next steps of financial development, including the introduction of a local currency bond market, could take place without disrupting the availability of foreign exchange.

In addition, a foreign exchange hedging tool could provide supplemental incentives for banks to channel excess U.S. dollar liquidity into riel-denominated NCDs. By engaging in sell-buy dollar swap contracts, banks could guarantee themselves cash flows in dollar terms. The riel-denominated NCDs combined with swap contracts could effectively serve as convertible securities, which might be in high demand even by banks with excess dollar liquidity.

However, with virtually no activity for wholesale transactions, it is unlikely that the private swaps market would automatically emerge. Indeed, the limited riel liquidity may not be sufficient to support the buy-sell leg of the swap contract. The NBC could consider bridging this gap by offering an open swaps facility, available only to buyers of riel-denominated NCDs, and by acting as the primary lender of riels to promote the new securities. Against the potential benefits of such an initiative, however, one must also take into account the added market complexity, pricing difficulties, uncertain fiscal burden, and credibility costs.[4]

SEQUENCING THE INITIATIVES

The choice of policy initiatives at the disposal of the NBC to drive financial development largely depends on the pace and depth that the authorities choose to undertake dedollarization. The initiatives, as shown in Table 8.1, can be divided into three components: (i) financial development policies, (ii) monetary policy tools, and (iii) regulatory and other measures. These initiatives are collectively the nuts and bolts that, if introduced and implemented in the right sequence, will combine to create an efficient financial market infrastructure and an independent monetary policy framework. Several alternative sequences are outlined next to highlight the issues involved in rolling out these initiatives. This is followed by a discussion of communications strategy, something that is essential to overcome potential coordination failure and to induce households and firms to jointly make greater use of the local currency.

Strategy 1: A Dual Approach

Under Strategy 1, the first milestone would be the introduction of NCDs as new securities in both currencies, with a phase-out schedule for the existing fixed deposit facility (see Figure 8.2). The announced commitment to phase out the old facility should help develop the new interbank market by promoting subscription and liquidity in the secondary market, especially at the early stage. Market activity for NCDs in dollars is expected to dominate initially, and this may help sustain or even increase the already extensive degree of financial dollarization. The

[4]Since there is no benchmark for market swap rates, the NBC would need to dictate the terms of the swaps. A more favorable rate could sweeten the NCDs and boost demand for them, but at a fiscal cost in terms of the impact on the NBC's balance sheet. By taking the buy-sell leg, the NBC could also stand to gain from any depreciation in riels, which might adversely affect the NBC's credibility in promoting the stability of the local currency.

TABLE 8.1

Types of Initiatives

Initiatives	Elements
Financial development	• Stock market • Collateralized interbank market • Wholesale foreign exchange (FX) market • Local currency bond market • Basic derivatives
Monetary policy	• Reserve requirement (RR) • Exchange rate policy • Liquidity management/open market operations (OMO) • Communication by monetary policy committee (MPC)
Regulations/ Other	• Pricing/settlement convention • Remuneration on required reserves • Remuneration on fixed deposit facility • Deposit insurance

government should therefore state at the outset its comprehensive dedollarization strategy and clarify that, once the economy makes sufficient progress in dedollarization, the dollar-denominated NCDs will no longer be issued.

The second milestone of this strategy would comprise a number of specific incentives to promote and strengthen the credibility of the overall dedollarization plan. The key objective at this stage is to propel the economy away from the current state of near-complete dollarization and create a significant boost of riel volume in the financial system. As a crude benchmark, the target could be to achieve riel deposits of 20 percent of total deposits, a level similar to that in other highly dollarized economies.

Key measures would include (i) widening the reserve requirement's ratio gap between foreign and domestic currencies;[5] (ii) remunerating required reserves for riel deposits and lowering remuneration for dollar deposits;[6] and (iii) providing deposit insurance to riel deposits. The first two measures are taxes on dollar intermediation and could serve to reduce financial dollarization. The third initiative strengthens the riel's function as a store of value, helps reverse asset substitution, and also ultimately promotes currency substitution. The potential cost of the latter measure should initially be low, in line with the amount of riel deposits in the system, whereas any incentive distortion (e.g., with regard to competition among banks) could be curbed by limiting the amount of deposit insurance provided.

[5]The prevailing economic developments would dictate how the widening should be engineered. If there is a need for overall monetary policy tightening, the NBC could raise the reserve requirement relatively more for foreign currency deposits. On the other hand, a more policy-neutral option would be to simultaneously raise the reserve requirement for foreign currency and lower that for riel. Currently, there is ample room for lowering the riel reserve requirement, which stands at 8 percent.

[6]As of June 2013, the reserve requirement on foreign currency deposits was 12.5 percent. Any required reserve for dollars in excess of the pre-2008 level of 8 percent is remunerated at half the SIBOR rate, with the rest not remunerated. The remuneration on required reserves is a relatively recent initiative, adopted when the reserve requirement on foreign currency deposits was raised for the first time in 2008.

Figure 8.2 Strategy 1: Dual approach

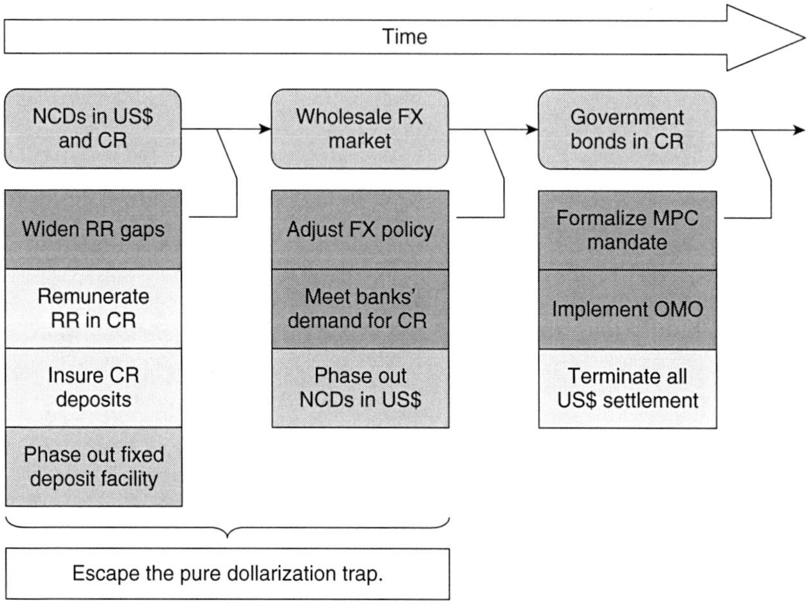

Note: CR = Cambodian riel; FX = foreign exchange; MPC = monetary policy committee; NCDs = negotiable certificates of deposit; OMO = open market operations; RR = reserve requirement.

A third milestone would be to put in place a wholesale foreign exchange market infrastructure, capable of matching sizable flows among institutional participants. As the degree of financial dollarization is progressively reduced, the volume of larger-scale foreign exchange transactions will rise. As the volume for NCDs in riels rises, there will be an opportunity to develop active foreign exchange forward and swap markets. The availability of foreign exchange hedging instruments, by lowering exchange rate risk, should further raise demand for riel-denominated securities. The government could possibly accelerate the pace of financial dedollarization by gradually phasing out the dollar-denominated NCDs, allowing riel-denominated NCDs to serve as the collateral for interbank lending in dollars, with appropriate haircuts or other hedges against embedded exchange rate risks.

As both asset and cash substitution begin to reverse, the NBC can accommodate higher structural demand for riels by calibrating foreign exchange policy to curb excessive appreciation of the currency. This is an opportunity for the NBC to accumulate more foreign reserves without adding to inflationary pressure, which can be achieved by ensuring that the injection of riel liquidity is gradual, consistent with market demand, and does not lead to large swings in the money market interest rate. A small appreciation of the riel could also be allowed, which would lend further impetus to dedollarization, creating a self-reinforcing process. At this stage, the NBC would also need to begin managing riel liquidity actively through a repurchase operation involving riel-denominated NCDs in order to tighten control over short-term interest rates, thus laying the groundwork for possible open market operations.

Once the riel money market and the foreign exchange market are both well established, the next step is to introduce longer-maturity government securities. Developing the public debt market in domestic currency and extending the yield curve would help promote the development of other financial markets (including basic derivatives such as interest rate swaps), which have proven to be an important catalyst for dedollarization in other countries such as Peru (see Garcia-Escribano, 2010). A yield curve would also serve as a transmission mechanism for market-based monetary policy. To this end, the NBC should prepare for such a transition by formalizing a monetary policy framework (objectives, instruments, and targets). By explicitly tying monetary policy to a domestic nominal anchor, the new framework will lend further credibility to macroeconomic policy management, another boost to dedollarization. After sufficient progress is made, the settlement of all banking transactions in dollars could then be terminated.

The key risk of Strategy 1 is that the measures introduced in the first step could fail to induce a substantial shift away from the near-complete dollarization. Falling short of making some progress in this crucial step, the dollar-denominated NCDs could end up bolstering financial dollarization. In that case, phasing them out subsequently might not only be a step backward for financial development, but also constitute a setback to the authorities' credibility. Issuing NCDs in dollars could also cast doubt on their commitment to dedollarize the economy.

Strategy 2: Dedollarization as Prerequisite

Strategy 2 considers an alternative sequencing, in which only the riel-denominated NCDs are issued initially as new securities. At the start, the demand for the riel-denominated NCDs is likely to be very low, mirroring banks' current portfolio allocation. Consequently, banks may continue to manage their dollar liquidity through the existing fixed deposit facility. Because banks do not have alternative means of managing their dollar liquidity, the NBC may have no option but to keep the old facility available, until the volume for NCDs in riels has risen sufficiently to be useful as collateral for interbank activity in dollars. However, without an explicit phase-out period, banks would have little incentive to stop relying on the fixed deposit facility and switch to subscribing to NCDs in riels. Thus, money market development might be a more protracted process under this strategy, requiring a more forceful implementation of accompanying dedollarization measures (second milestone under Strategy 1) to further the process of financial development (see Figure 8.3).

What the second strategy buys is insurance that the financial development plan does nothing to jeopardize the dedollarization policy, since the financial markets are developed exclusively in riel denomination. The flip-side is that successful dedollarization becomes a precondition for further progress in financial development. Under the second strategy, only when the extent of financial dedollarization sufficiently declines will the volume of NCDs rise, enabling the riel-denominated NCDs to serve as collateral for both riel- and any remaining

Figure 8.3 Strategy 2: Riel NCDs only

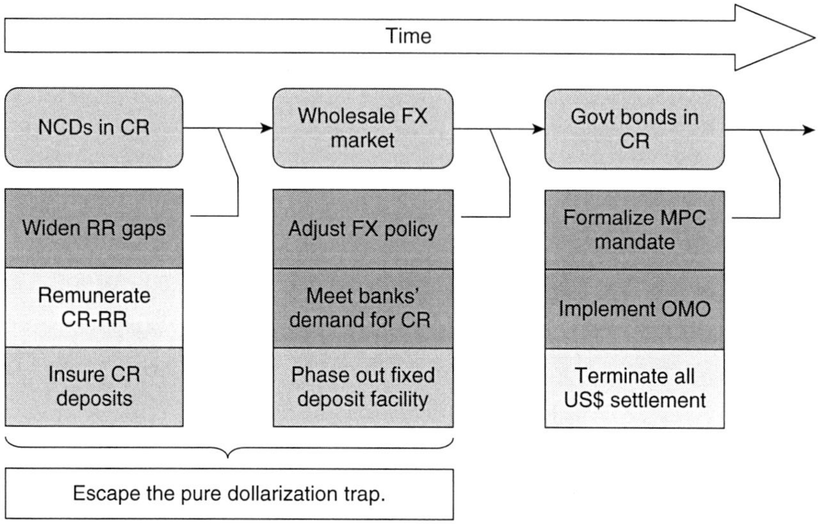

Note: CR = Cambodian riel; FX = foreign exchange; MPC = monetary policy committee; NCDs = negotiable certificates of deposit; OMO = open market operations; RR = reserve requirement.

dollar-denominated interbank loans. With an interbank market reasonably active in both currencies, a wholesale foreign exchange market could then be developed along with foreign exchange hedging tools. The ability to hedge foreign exchange risks would raise the potential of using riel-denominated NCDs as collateral for dollar-denominated loans and the fixed deposit facility could then be phased out gradually. With an interbank market firmly established, the next steps of developing a debt market and creating a new monetary policy framework can then proceed as in Strategy 1. As discussed earlier (under capital and foreign exchange markets), the NBC could augment the initial stage of this approach by introducing an official swap facility that hedges foreign exchange rate risk for buyers of NCDs in riels. The design of such a facility itself poses important challenges (e.g., regarding term and rate structure), but the facility could be a catalyst for accelerating the demand for riel-denominated NCDs.

A Gradual Approach

The two strategies discussed so far represent distinct cases that may not be optimally aligned with the NBC's preferences regarding the two objectives of dedollarization and financial development. For example, in practice the authorities may want to ensure the success of dedollarization with a very high probability, but at the same time they may be unwilling to trade off the postponement of financial development indefinitely.

A third strategy could combine Strategies 1 and 2. Under this hybrid strategy, the NCDs could initially be issued exclusively in riels, similar to Strategy 2.

However, if no material progress were subsequently observed in interbank market development, a small amount of dollar-denominated NCDs could be issued to boost market activity. The issuance size of NCDs in dollars could be capped below the full market demand and be allowed to increase only gradually and only to the extent that it did not exacerbate the degree of financial dollarization. The fixed deposit facility could continue to exist, but a limit would need to be placed on its size, too, which in turn could be reduced over time.

Under this hybrid strategy, the authorities would retain firm control over the dedollarization objective. The strategy would send a strong signal about their commitment, afford a more gradual transition from the old to the new regime, and still allow greater benefits from financial development. During the gradual transition, any effect on dollarization could also be monitored. Should the degree of dollarization intensify or remain high, the authorities would need to consider strengthening the incentive measures to encourage greater use of the riel and/or scale down the issuance of NCDs in dollars. The opportunity to fine-tune policy measures as warranted without compromising policy credibility is another benefit of this approach.

The key challenge in this case is still to break away from the near-complete dollarized state, so the implementation of broader dedollarization policies through regulatory and other policy tools should remain a top priority. Without these measures, there would be little impetus for the demand of riel securities to take off, and a large-scale financial dollarization would likely persist.

Communication

The dollarization phenomenon and the general choice of currency are partly driven by coordination failure. While a systemwide switch to the Cambodian riel may be beneficial for the society as a whole, each individual has little incentive to switch unless others are also willing to change their choice of currency. The perceived likelihood of a successful dedollarization is not only a measure of policy credibility, but could potentially be self-fulfilling.

The authorities can leverage the self-fulfilling nature of public expectations and lend further support to the dedollarization process by communicating clearly and strategically about their plans and objectives. Some key messages to be conveyed include the following:

- The NBC is committed to dedollarization in a deep and stable financial system based on the riel and to an independent monetary policy that can propel the economy into its next stage of development.
- The process of financial development is itself driven by a set of carefully sequenced and comprehensive initiatives to achieve this objective.
- The initiatives will encourage greater use of riels both for ordinary transactions and within the financial system, broadening the existing policy scope, which has so far been focused on dedollarizing the real sector.
- Both individual households and financial institutions can benefit from greater asset diversification toward riel use, given the authorities' commitment

(i) to keep the local currency strong through stable macroeconomic conditions; and (ii) to develop the financial markets with the riel playing a prominent role. Additionally, risk-adjusted riel funding costs would likely fall.

CONCLUSION

Financial market development and dedollarization are both important policy objectives in Cambodia that cannot be pursued independently of each other. Rather than prioritizing one objective over the other, this chapter discusses how an appropriate sequencing of measures within a coherent strategy can help reduce the tension and pursue both financial development and dedollarization simultaneously. A fully developed strategy would serve as a concrete policy vision for the NBC in moving toward an efficient and independent monetary framework, while at the same time helping to enhance policy credibility.

REFERENCES

Asel, Isakova, 2010, "Financial Sector Development and Dollarization in the Economies of Central Asia," Unpublished paper (London: European Bank for Reconstruction and Development; Center for Economic Research and Graduate Education—Economics Institute).

De Nicolo, Gianni, Patrick Honohan, and Alain Ize, 2003, "Dollarization of the Banking System: Good or Bad?" Policy Research Working Paper No. 3116 (Washington: World Bank).

De Zamaróczy, Mario, and Sopanha Sa, 2002, "Macroeconomic Adjustment in a Highly Dollarized Economy: The Case of Cambodia," IMF Working Paper No. 02/92 (Washington: International Monetary Fund).

Garcia-Escribano, Mercedes, 2010, "Peru: Drivers of Dedollarization," IMF Working Paper No. 10/169 (Washington: International Monetary Fund).

Ize, Alain, and Eduardo Levy Yeyati, 2003, "Financial Dollarization," *Journal of International Economics,* Vol. 59, pp. 323–47.

Royal Government of Cambodia, 2012 "Financial Sector Development Strategy 2011–2020" (Phnom Penh).

Yeyati, E. Levy, 2005, "Financial Dollarization: Evaluating the Consequences," Presentation to the 41st Panel Meeting of Economic Policy, Luxembourg, April 15–16, 2005.

CHAPTER 9

Modernizing Supervision in Support of Stable Financial Development

RODOLFO MAINO

Safeguarding the stability of Cambodia's rapidly evolving financial system requires more coordinated and forward-looking supervision. The National Bank of Cambodia (NBC) has strengthened the regulatory framework, taken a stricter stance on bank licensing, and restructured its banking supervision. It has also addressed credit risks by introducing a new credit reporting system coinciding with the launching of a credit information bureau. However, a crisis management framework encompassing key financial supervisors is yet to be fully developed, and supervisory capacity remains stretched.

In this chapter we review the milestones achieved in recent years and key issues going forward in developing a financial supervision function commensurate with Cambodia's increasingly diverse and interconnected financial system.

CAMBODIA'S FINANCIAL SYSTEM: MOVING BEYOND BANKS

Banking Institutions

Cambodia has a bank-centric financial system (Figure 9.1). After the abolition of the use of money and banking by the Khmer Rouge in the late 1970s, banks reentered the system in the 1980s under a mono-bank framework typical for centrally planned economies. In 1989, a multilayered system was introduced with the NBC at the helm, and commercial bank functions were separated from the NBC. The financial system has witnessed rapid growth since 2006 (Table 9.1), although the scope for further financial deepening remains large, since the broader economy remains cash-based, especially in rural areas.

As discussed in detail in Chapter 4, Cambodia's banking system has a concentrated structure and significant foreign presence (Table 9.1). As of end-2012, the "big five" banks held almost 60 percent of total banking sector assets and accounted for the same share of net credit from the banking sector. Together, the foreign-owned banks held 45 percent of total assets and 40 percent of total deposits. With the rural economy largely cash-based, most of the banks in Cambodia

Figure 9.1 Structure of the Financial Sector, 2010

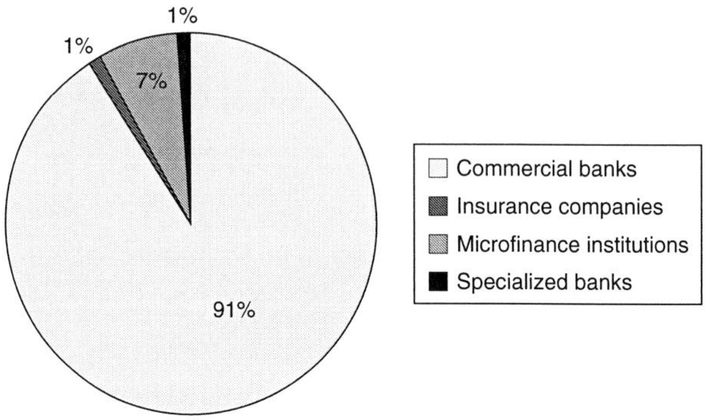

Source: National Bank of Cambodia.

TABLE 9.1
Cambodia: Banking Institutions

	Number of Institutions						
Type of Institution	**2006**	**2007**	**2008**	**2009**	**2010**	**2011**	**2012**
Total number of banks	20	24	30	33	36	38	39
Commercial banks	15	17	24	27	30	31	32
Foreign branch banks	3	3	3	5	7	9	9
Locally incorporated	12	14	21	22	23	22	23
Specialized banks	5	7	6	6	6	7	7
State-owned	1	1	1	1	1	1	1
Privately owned	4	6	5	5	5	6	6
Microfinance institutions	16	17	18	26	25	32	36
Representative offices	2	2	2	2	2	2	4

Source: National Bank of Cambodia.

operate in urban centers such as Phnom Penh—albeit the largest banks have already started to develop regional networks. As a result, most banks are competing for market share with a limited range of products. The rapid growth in the number of banks that has occurred along with this structure not only poses challenges to financial stability, as highlighted in Chapter 4, but also stretches the NBC's supervisory capacity to assess credit expansion, loan portfolio quality, risk management, operational risk, and profitability—which are the focus of this chapter.

Microfinance Institutions

Among financial institutions, microfinance institutions are witnessing rapid growth and have the widest distribution networks in rural areas. Some of the fast-growing ones are entering into the commercial banking area. The loan portfolios of the 35 registered microfinance institutions exceeded US$1 billion (about one-fifth of the banks' total loan portfolio) and grew by 41 percent (year-over-year) by March 2013.

Although these institutions relied heavily on external sources to fund their growth in the past, they are now relying increasingly on domestic funding.[1]

Insurance Sector

The Cambodian insurance market is small and has a nascent life insurance segment. There are currently six insurers, including two bank subsidiaries, one reinsurer,[2] and one life insurance company that started operation in 2012.[3] The sector's total assets stood at around US$86 million and its total premiums at about US$30 million in 2011, which accounted for a mere 0.9 percent and 0.3 percent of GDP, respectively. Although it started from a low base, the industry is growing steadily, reflecting an increase in the utilization of insurance and the relocalization of businesses previously abroad. The entry of new insurance companies has also contributed to increased competition, the introduction of new operating models, and reductions in premium costs.[4]

Securities Market

The development of capital markets in Cambodia is still in an embryonic stage. Markets for corporate debt and government debt securities do not yet exist. A stock market opened in April 2012, but currently only one company is listed there. The stock market's development is part of a road map adopted by the government, which contains strategies for developing the financial sector from 2011 to 2020. To this end, the Cambodian authorities have entered into a strategic alliance with the Korean Stock Exchange, which aims to have around 40 listed companies registered on the Cambodian Securities Exchange over the next five years. In addition, the Cambodian Mercantile Exchange is to serve as an organized exchange for the buying and selling of commodities as well as derivative products. To implement these strategies, the country needs to actively promote market development, including by improving accounting and auditing practices; correcting deficiencies in the judicial system; strengthening the legal infrastructure; increasing technical capacity among market participants and supervisors; and further developing broad-based financial literacy.

Foreign Exchange Market

It is expected that the stock market will over time increase the supply and demand for foreign exchange, especially given Cambodia's open capital account and

[1]Seven microfinance institutions are currently licensed to take deposits. These deposits reached US$346 million in March 2013, increasing by 145 percent in the preceding 12 months.

[2]The reinsurer is a joint venture between the Ministry of Economy and Finance (MEF) and a regional insurance group.

[3]Cambodian Life Insurance Company Plc. (Cambodian Life) is a joint venture established on January 10, 2012 by Cambodia's MEF and four other partners.

[4]So far, reported industry level profitability has been largely maintained. Claims ratios are low and underwriting profits continue to be healthy. Further growth will depend on innovative approaches in products and distribution to the underserved Cambodian population.

growing foreign investor interest. However, the foreign exchange market currently lacks the ability to manage large capital flows. It is centered on licensed money changers, with commercial banks playing a minor role.[5] Moreover, the NBC is currently constraining exchange rate flexibility in a very thin market, either by dealing directly with large customers or by regularly auctioning foreign exchange to clear the retail spot market, which impinges on the development of the foreign exchange market.

Deepening the foreign exchange market will likely require the NBC to gradually step back from the market by dealing less with retail money changers and more with banks, while also allowing some flexibility in the exchange rate to give the foreign exchange market a chance of clearing itself. This enhanced flexibility should be carefully sequenced with progress in developing the monetary framework, as discussed in the previous chapter. The NBC could also review the possibility of offering foreign exchange swaps of riels for dollars to help encourage the development of a forward foreign exchange market (see Box 9.1).

FINANCIAL SYSTEM SOUNDNESS AND REFORM

Cambodia's financial system transformation will continue to play an important role in the country's economic development. The current goals for the financial sector are framed in a road map for its development over the period 2011–2020;[6] they are complemented by the findings and recommendations of the 2010 IMF-World Bank Financial Sector Assessment Program (FSAP). The ultimate objective of this master plan is the development of a sound market-based financial system to support resource mobilization, effective financial resource allocation, and broad-based sustainable economic growth.

Along with a steady transformation of the Cambodian economy since the 1980s, the legal framework and supervisory and regulatory regimes have been further developed to provide effective recourse against financial sector risks. Nonetheless, progress in implementing high-priority 2010 FSAP recommendations has been uneven (Table 9.2). On the one hand, a higher minimum capital requirement for banks was delivered as scheduled and noncompliant banks are being dealt with, while the NBC is continuing to upgrade its supervisory capacity. The recent update of the national payments system (Box 9.2) and the launch of the credit information bureau have encouraged better risk management in the system. On the other hand, work on key elements of a crisis management framework remains at an initial stage. Agreement on the delineation of responsibilities among different supervisors is still pending, while the NBC's supervisory capacity remains stretched. This section will review progress in key areas, while the following section outlines future reform challenges.

---

[5]At present, there are 12 licensed money changers that are at the core of the foreign exchange market and 2,547 accredited money changers, who deal with very small cash transactions. Among these 12 licensed money changers, four or five dominate the market and manage large transaction flows.

[6]Available via the Internet: http://www.nbc.org.kh/english/publications/blueprints.php

BOX 9.1

Toward a Deeper and More Resilient Foreign Exchange Market

An active foreign exchange market would boost financial sector development by building trust among banks and by providing basic infrastructure and liquidity for further financial market development, for example by smoothly intermediating foreign capital flows related to expected growth in the volume of stock market transactions. The NBC is considering steps to make banks the primary participants in its auctions. The strategic goal is to gradually transition the foreign exchange market from one dominated by retail money changers to one dominated by wholesale banks. Moreover, the NBC should consider these points:

- In the first instance, the NBC should build a relationship with the foreign exchange divisions of the banks and advise them to participate in the NBC's auctions.
- Over time, the NBC could look to tighten the criteria applied to eligible participants in its foreign exchange auctions with a view to limiting participation to the banks and the large money changers who meet prudential guidelines. The objective is to place the banks at the center of the market and have retail customers and money changers deal with the banks, which would then deal with the NBC, if necessary. The central bank law suggests that only "financial institutions" should deal with the NBC (Article 5 of the NBC law) and that money changers do not meet the definition of a financial institution. This strategy could also interact with and support the authorities' intentions to dedollarize the economy.
- This approach could take the form of a primary dealer system, in which primary dealers have the right to come to the NBC and participate in their auctions and interventions. The privilege of being primary dealers could come with some obligations. For example, there might be requirements for them to regularly report information on market developments and market turnover to the NBC. In addition, it is common for primary dealers to be required to quote prices to other interbank wholesale market participants and to customers. This sort of measure is useful in bringing depth to the market.

In addition, the NBC could consider:

- *Promoting the development of foreign exchange brokers*. The NBC should look at developing a role for foreign exchange brokers by setting up a relevant broker licensing regime, seeking guidance from the Securities and Exchange Commission of Cambodia (SECC), as brokers currently exist in the equity market.
- *Developing foreign exchange hedging tools*. Some very basic foreign exchange products are not available in Cambodia, but they will be needed to allow (i) the Cambodian market to be able to handle the capital flows associated with the opening of the equity market, and (ii) the NBC to step back from the market.
- *Encouraging the development of a foreign exchange (currency) swap market* which would then enable foreign exchange forward transactions to occur. In the global foreign exchange market, foreign exchange swaps, forwards, and spot foreign exchange are the three most important foreign exchange hedging products traded. This would necessitate developing the interbank market and the market for NBC securities. The NBC has periodically transacted foreign exchange swaps with banks through the format of a U.S. dollar-collateralized riel loan from the NBC. The foreign exchange swap market can provide a money market benchmark interest rate in its own right, which can be useful for the conduct of monetary policy, thus aiding dedollarization and providing the market with riels that can be used to purchase riel-denominated NBC securities.

BOX 9.2

Payment Systems

In December 2012, the NBC launched a new National Clearing System to further facilitate the clearing of checks and the distribution of cash through 21 branches located in the provinces. Membership in the Clearing House currently stands at 32 institutions for U.S. dollar clearing and 26 for riel clearing. Other relevant participants in the payment services provision are microfinance institutions.

Cash is the predominant means of payment in Cambodia (see also Chapter 3). Two currencies dominate the market: the Cambodian riel and the U.S. dollar. In certain areas of the country, where Cambodia and Thailand share a border, the Thai baht is also in use. Most of the population's payroll is paid in cash. Until recently, even large purchases were completed in cash. The use of the riel is generally limited to small routine purchases, government purchases, payment of taxes and utilities, and banks required to hold reserves in accounts at the NBC. Checks are the second most common form of payment instrument in the country, aided by the successful introduction of some new checking standards within Cambodia's banking system in 2012.

As of end-2012, there were only 406 automated teller machines (ATMs) in Cambodia and 3,300 point-of-sale terminals, but this represented an increase of over 130 percent since 2007. However, this structure introduces inefficiencies into the market, reduces the use of card services (because there are limits to where customers can access the services), creates barriers to entry for new service providers, and ultimately translates to increased costs to the consumers. However, there has been some, albeit limited, sharing of ATM networks by a few banks.

Cambodia's national payment system still requires substantive improvements to fully conform to international standards. There is a need to further strengthen the legal soundness of the payment system by completing the work that is under way on a new, overarching National Payment Systems Law. Once enacted, this law could reduce or eliminate the need for an individual *Prakas* (regulation). A well-formulated strategy to promote an electronic means of payment would help, too. Finally, the migration from paper-based instruments to electronic ones is a key element in increasing the efficiency of the payment system, potentially yielding real and noticeable benefits to bank customers and to the economy as a whole.

Improved Credit Risk Management by Banks

In February 2009, the NBC adopted a *Prakas* (regulation) on asset classification and provisioning that aimed to provide a better tool for portfolio assessment. This *Prakas* replaced a 2002 regulation, requiring that all loans and assets of banking and financial institutions be evaluated regularly using a risk-based and forward-looking method. In particular, the classification of all assets was updated from four (standard, substandard, doubtful, and loss) to five categories (normal, special mention, substandard, doubtful, and loss). Timely and appropriate provisions and write-offs were also required to build reserves for loan loss accounts in order to accurately reflect the true condition and operating results of the institutions. In

TABLE 9.2

Cambodia: Key 2010 FSAP Recommendations of High Priority

Recommendation	Time frame[1]	Status	Notes
	General Stability		
• Improve the quality of data to enable an appropriate assessment of risks, and to enhance the reliability of stress tests, including through strengthening supervision; and collecting additional credit-related information.	Short-term	In process	Structural project involving the NBC as well as the whole financial sector
• Ensure that banks retain an appropriate level of liquid assets to be able to meet short-term obligations by enforcing existing regulations.	Short-term	In process	Amendments to the *Prakas* already drafted
• Upgrade law to formalize delineation of responsibilities among supervisors, and establish procedures, through MoUs, for practical information exchange, coordination and accountability among domestic supervisors (NBC, MEF, SECC), and with foreign supervisors.	Short-term	Initiated but not concluded	In process with many foreign authorities but lagging with domestic supervisors
• Upgrade both the number and capacity of staff in the areas of banking, insurance, securities and payment system supervision; develop training programs for financial institutions on accounting, corporate governance, risk management, and for the external audit profession.	Medium-term	In process	-
• Develop and implement a strategic plan to address the conflicts and overlaps in the financial sector legal and regulatory framework.	Medium-term	In process	In cooperation with World Bank (WB)
	Supervision and Regulation		
Banking			
• Develop supervisory strategy to deal with banks that cannot meet the new capital requirement.	Short-term	Done	-
• Conduct comprehensive upgrades to the legal framework.	Short-term	In process	In cooperation with WB
• Reprioritize the work performed by the staff to facilitate forward-looking, risk-based supervision.	Short-term	In process	Action plan after reviewing compliance with BCPs
• Impose a moratorium on the issuance of new bank licenses as long as supervisory capacity and resources remain inadequate.	Short-term	Under NBC review	Stance tightened toward the issuance of licenses
Nonbank Financial Sector			
• Revise capital regulations in concert with liability, investment, and accounting rules to better reflect the risks in a growing insurance market.	Short-term	Done	-
• Enhance powers for intervention, corrective measures, and enforcement.	Short-term	In process	In cooperation with WB
• Conduct a readiness study prior to the launch of the stock exchange.	Short-term	Done	-

(*Continued*)

TABLE 9.2 ***(Continued)***

Recommendation	Time frame[1]	Status	Notes
Access to Finance			
• Enhance supervisory practices to keep pace with the development of microfinance deposit-taking institutions, and impose a moratorium as long as supervisory capacity and resources remain inadequate.	Medium-term	In process	-
Crisis Management Framework			
• Revise PCA framework by developing additional triggers for asset quality, liquidity, and earlier intervention based on the solvency ratio.	Medium-term	In preparation	In cooperation with WB
• Introduce regulation allowing banks to use their fixed deposits at the NBC and any issue of government (including government bodies) or government-guaranteed securities as eligible collateral for interbank and NBC repos.	Short-term	In process	Project for issuing NBC's negotiable certificates of deposits
• Develop a crisis management framework.	Medium-term	In preparation	In cooperation with WB
Transparency of Monetary and Financial Policies			
• Introduce due process for the dismissal of NBC Board members and the Governor by specifying the legal grounds for doing so, and defining an appeal process.	Medium-term	Not initiated	To be considered with the assistance of WB
• Amend the law to reduce the government's representation on the Board of the NBC; and to reflect the practice of appointing two Deputy Governors.	Short-term	Not initiated	To be considered with the assistance of WB
Corporate governance of banks			
• Draft and/or implement banking regulations on internal audit and controls, risk management, and compliance functions at banks.	Short-term	Done	-
Anti-Money Laundering and Combating Financing of Terrorism (AML/CFT)			
• Introduce new rules measures for conducting overall AML/CFT risk assessments and risk profiling of financial institutions.	Short-term	Not initiated	To be considered with the Financial Intelligence Unit

Note: FSAP = the IMF-World Bank Financial Sector Assessment Program. BCPs = Basel Core Principles for Effective Banking Supervision; MEF = Ministry of Economy and Finance; MoUs = memoranda of understanding; NBC = National Bank of Cambodia; PCA = prompt corrective action; SECC = Securities and Exchange Commission of Cambodia.

[1]Short-term: up to one year; medium term: one–three years. Status of implementation as of May 2013.

addition, in September 2010, the NBC issued a *Prakas* on internal control, aiming at supporting the implementation of risk-based and forward-looking supervision and achieving compliance with the Basel Core Principles for Effective Banking Supervision. The organization and the efficiency of these internal control systems are assessed by the NBC's Banking Supervision Department—both its off-site and on-site divisions—as well by the banks themselves in a dedicated annual report submitted to the NBC. Indeed, for over two years, banking institutions in Cambodia have implemented their own internal control systems, adjusting their risk management processes and mitigating operational risks and supervisory concerns.

In addition, the introduction of a new credit reporting system signals a key effort to deal with credit risks. In May 2011, the NBC adopted a *Prakas* to establish a credit reporting system (CRS). It requires that all financial institutions in Cambodia, defined by the Law on Banking and Financial Institutions and approved by the NBC, contribute the credit information to the CRS. The new reporting system is updated monthly and available online, which is crucial to improving the timeliness and accuracy of information reporting and to reducing the burden and cost related to previous paper reporting submissions. Moreover, the NBC now has the authority to set up relevant regulations, to monitor all credit reporting activities, to oversee the CRS, and to issue licenses to Credit Reporting System Service Providers.

In line with the introduction of the CRS, the Credit Bureau of Cambodia was launched in March 2012. With all the banks, regulated microfinance institutions, and three unregulated entities as its members, the credit bureau provides access to personal credit histories and makes it possible for different financial institutions to access customer information on a common platform. It also helps to alleviate the concerns of overlapping loans, particularly among small lenders, and thus to mitigate the credit risks.[7] With electronic data submissions from all covered entities, the Credit Bureau of Cambodia is currently the single Credit Reporting System Service Provider for the CRS, and is now working on creating a commercial bureau (company database).

Transition to Risk-Based Supervision by the NBC

The NBC has made progress in transitioning from compliance-based to risk-based supervision. The supervision department has started to conduct risk forecasting on individual banks and on a consolidated basis. Off-site examination teams have begun to compile risk profiles to be used for making on-site inspection plans. A working group was formed to review compliance with the Basel Core Principles and has concluded a first detailed assessment. Specifically:

- The NBC issued a *Prakas* in February 2011 announcing the transition from compliance-based supervision to risk-based and forward-looking supervision. The *Prakas* stressed that (i) the NBC will implement risk-based and forward-looking supervisory monitoring aimed at anticipating potential adverse

[7]The increasing usage of reports from the Credit Bureau of Cambodia is transforming the risk landscape in the formal financial system by helping banks and microfinancial institutions avoid riskier loans, some of which are shifting to the informal sector and shadow banking activity. The number of credit inquiries increased from 6,000 to 158,000 a month (of which 30,000 were from banks) in the 12 months to February 2013.

developments and at addressing them in a timely manner; (ii) the supervisory monitoring processes will be based on risk-profile assessments, examinations' findings and extrapolations, and stress testing; and (iii) the NBC will perform comprehensive risk-profile assessments at the banking institution level and also, where applicable, at the consolidated level.

- The new banking supervision system has started to take shape with the support of external technical assistance. A template has been used to conduct risk forecasting both on an individual bank level and on a consolidated level. On-site inspection plans are being made based on the compiling of risk assessments by the off-site department. A working group was also set up in 2011 to review the Basel Core Principles. Following the completion of the review, a program was developed aiming to comply with the principles. A detailed assessment of compliance with the Basel principles has been summarized and submitted to the senior NBC management. Following broad compliance with the Pillar I standardized approach, the NBC is now working toward full implementation of Basel II (the second accord on recommendations on banking laws and regulations issued by the Basel Committee on Banking Supervision).

THE ROAD AHEAD: FUTURE CHALLENGES

Achieving the above milestones now provides a solid basis for ongoing reforms. Meeting higher minimum capital requirements and adopting stricter enforcement of new regulations on asset classification and provisioning have buttressed the NBC's credibility as a supervisor, as have the regulations for risk-based and forward-looking supervision. That an adequate regulatory and supervisory framework for the securities market is being developed as well is also valuable. Financial soundness indicators for banks presently do not seem to point to immediate financial stability risks over the medium term (Table 9.3). Nevertheless, the supervisory framework needs to keep pace with the development of a broader financial system, which means that modalities are needed to enhance cooperation and coordination between the NBC and other domestic supervisors. From a supervisory perspective, two main challenges to financial system stability stand out:

- *Supervisory capacity.* Against the backdrop of a rapidly developing banking system, the NBC is addressing its human resources and technical capacity constraints, including through the training and hiring of new recruits. In addition, technical assistance continues to play an important role in knowledge transfer as the NBC seeks to upgrade its surveillance of financial stability risks (e.g., stress testing).
- *Crisis management framework.* This will be critical to help maintain confidence in the financial system and minimize fiscal risks. The "prompt corrective action" regulation for the NBC needs to be strengthened, given the absence of financial safety nets. The crisis management framework will also

TABLE 9.3

Cambodia: Core Financial Soundness Indicators (FSIs), 2008–11 *(In percent)*

	2008	2009				2010				2011				2012	
	Dec.	Mar.	Jun.	Sep.	Dec.	Mar.	Jun.	Sep.	Dec.	Mar.	Jun.	Sep.	Dec.	Mar.	Jun.
Capital-based FSIs															
Regulatory capital to risk-weighted assets	27.6	32.4	33.1	34.2	32.3	31.5	31.3	31.5	31.4	31.2	29.0	27.5	26.2	29.1	28.8
Regulatory Tier 1 capital to risk-weighted assets	27.7	32.8	37.2	34.8	33.0	32.7	33.3	32.6	32.1	29.5	27.7	26.3	26.3	29.3	28.9
Nonperforming loans net of provisions to capital	5.9	8.2	8.3	9.7	5.3	5.1	5.5	6.0	3.8	3.9	4.6	5.4	3.3	3.8	3.5
Return on equity[1]	12.4	5.8	5.0	4.7	4.9	5.9	6.2	6.6	6.5	9.0	9.6	10.5	9.7	11.2	11.0
Net open position in foreign exchange to capital	0.9	0.9	1.0	4.5	1.4	3.2	5.0	5.0	2.3	3.1	3.0	3.9	3.9	2.9	3.4
Asset-based FSIs															
Nonperforming loans to total gross loans	2.9	4.3	4.9	5.7	3.9	4.1	4.2	4.2	2.9	2.9	3.0	3.0	2.1	2.4	2.2
Return on assets[1]	2.7	1.2	1.1	1.0	1.0	1.2	1.2	1.3	1.3	1.9	1.8	2.0	1.8	2.3	2.1
Liquid assets to total assets	14.2	15.4	16.2	19.8	19.4	16.1	18.0	17.6	18.0	17.9	17.9	19.0	16.2	17.2	17.5
Liquid assets to short-term liabilities	30.6	20.8	22.4	27.3	26.8	22.4	24.8	24.5	25.2	25.2	25.3	27.0	23.0	24.3	24.4
Sectoral distribution of loans to total gross loans															
Residents	94.4	95.1	97.8	94.7	95.0	91.7	92.1	91.8	91.8	91.0	90.8	91.1	92.3	88.3	85.7
Deposit-takers	3.8	3.5	4.5	5.9	6.5	6.6	6.1	4.0	4.4	3.9	4.7	4.9	7.7	8.1	7.9
Central bank	0.0	0.0	0.0	0.0	0.0	0.0	0.0	0.0	0.0	0.0	0.0	0.0	0.0	0.0	0.0
Other financial corporations	0.0	0.0	0.0	0.0	0.0	0.0	0.0	0.0	0.0	0.0	0.0	0.0	0.0	0.0	0.0
General government	0.0	0.0	0.0	0.0	0.0	0.0	0.0	0.0	0.0	0.0	0.0	0.0	0.0	0.0	0.0
Nonfinancial corporations	70.6	72.4	74.4	71.3	71.1	68.9	69.2	72.4	72.3	72.2	71.3	71.1	69.5	65.8	63.8
Other domestic sectors	20.1	19.3	18.9	17.5	17.5	16.2	16.8	15.4	15.1	14.9	14.8	15.1	15.1	14.4	14.0
Nonresidents	5.6	4.9	2.2	5.3	5.0	8.3	7.9	8.2	8.2	9.0	9.2	8.9	7.7	11.7	14.3
Income- and expense-based FSIs															
Interest margin to gross income	48.3	67.0	66.4	64.1	60.8	68.9	67.8	67.9	62.2	67.7	65.3	63.6	64.3	63.1	65.6
Noninterest expenses to gross income	64.2	65.4	66.9	65.4	64.2	65.3	62.9	61.2	63.2	56.8	57.9	56.1	57.5	53.9	54.7

Source: National Bank of Cambodia

[1]Annualized.

need to establish a mechanism for dealing with systemic and illiquid or insolvent banks. An explicit financial stability mandate for the NBC is also needed, while memoranda of understanding (MoUs) between Cambodia's three supervisory agencies (the NBC, the Ministry of Economy and Finance, and the SECC) are needed to avoid gaps in information sharing and responsibilities for crisis resolution. Moreover, deposit insurance, an important feature of a financial safety net, is absent, and depositors' claims are not accorded adequate priority.

These two challenges will be discussed in detail in the remainder of this chapter.

Supervisory and Licensing Capacity

A confluence of factors gives rise to supervisory capacity constraints:

- Institutionally, the Banking Supervision General Directorate of the NBC needs to attract and retain more qualified staff to effectively supervise the dynamic financial sector, including through competitive remuneration and adequate control over the directorate's own resources and hiring decisions. The directorate also needs to ensure that staff has sufficiently long tenure in the department to deepen specialized knowledge.
- The introduction of risk-based supervision imposes a higher demand on qualified staff to conduct risk-profile assessments, on-site and off-site examinations, analyses of findings, and stress-testing, and thus further strains the supervisory capacity.

Overall, notwithstanding an improvement in the quality of supervision, the relative shortage of staff, particularly the more experienced and qualified staff, has become a more binding constraint given the proliferation of banks and the introduction of risk-based supervision. However, the NBC has recently signed an MoU with foreign bank supervisors to improve supervisory collaboration. In light of the significant role of foreign-controlled banks in Cambodia, this step represents a potentially useful tool to ease capacity constraints and initiate cross-border supervision. In addition, the newly created Financial Stability Team of the NBC is an important capacity-building step.[8]

For as long as supervisory capacity remains relatively limited, a moratorium on new bank licenses, which was a key recommendation from the 2010 joint IMF-World Bank FSAP, remains applicable. The NBC has recently taken a more cautious stance toward the issuance of new licenses, including by encouraging potential applicants (domestic *and* foreign) to consider mergers with existing banks. To make bank licensing more stringent and transparent, the NBC should develop and document comprehensive criteria and guidelines for licensing and execute the power to reject applications that do not meet the standards. Considering the recent surge in foreign funding and the lack of constraints on foreign capital inflows into

---

[8]As part of its functions, the team now issues a quarterly Banking Stability Dashboard, a set of risk indicators for the financial system.

the country, the NBC's gatekeeper function of licensing needs to be strengthened rather than used as a means to attract foreign investment.[9] Along these lines, the BSD could also seek collaboration from the Consultative Supervisory Committee, which was established as an oversight committee within the NBC.

The effectiveness of efforts to improve supervisory and licensing capacity will also depend on improvements to the legal infrastructure (Box 9.3). For instance, the existing Law on Banking and Financial Institutions does not explicitly provide legal protection to the supervisory staff or the NBC from prosecution for the supervisory actions that they might take and all costs of defending their actions. The 2010 FSAP recommended that this law be amended and the legal framework be enhanced to incentivize the NBC to take prompt corrective actions effectively, and to empower the NBC to undertake a wider range of supervisory responses. Furthermore, to enhance the capability of off-site examination, technical assistance may be needed to support the Banking Supervision General Directorate team to conduct stress testing, particularly in the area of macro-financial linkages and scenario analysis skills.

Crisis Management Framework

In the absence of financial safety nets and given the very limited lender-of-last-resort capability of the NBC arising from Cambodia's high degree of dollarization (see Chapters 3 and 5), strengthening the financial crisis management framework remains key to reducing systemic risks. Financial stability arrangements involve multiple government entities and a set of explicit and implicit arrangements. The key players are the prudential supervisor, the central bank, the fiscal authority, and the deposit insurer, if any. Cambodia's recent economic upswing offers an opportune window to agree on MoUs among the NBC, the SECC, and the Ministry of Economy and Finance on establishing a coordinated supervision framework. A two-step approach has been initiated with a view to

- identifying areas where cooperation, including information sharing, can be readily achieved for the signing of an initial MoU that focuses on coordinated surveillance and crisis prevention; and
- agreeing on a time-bound process toward a second MoU on crisis resolution in order to complete the crisis management framework, with clearly defined roles and responsibilities of each supervisory agency (Ministry of Economy and Finance, SECC, and NBC).

Moving from process to substance, while the NBC has a broad understanding of the relevant roles and the nature of the response in the event of severe stress, the interagency crisis management framework requires a clear delineation of responsibilities, defined by (i) the apex crisis management committee, comprising the Governor of the NBC and the Minister of Economy and Finance; (ii) MoUs for

[9]In this context, going forward, bank flows and their sectoral destination, including to real estate, and their financial stability implications warrant closer monitoring.

cooperation and coordination among the regulators (among the Ministry of Economy and Finance, the NBC and the SECC, and with foreign supervisory/regulatory authorities); (iii) crisis management teams within the NBC and the Ministry of Economy and Finance; (iv) a crisis management manual with plans for addressing several contingencies; (v) a communication plan for the public; (vi) a market and institutional monitoring framework; and (vii) periodic crisis simulations.

Focusing on the role of the NBC, specifically in crisis resolution, the absence of an explicit financial stability mandate for the NBC constitutes an important gap. The NBC law defines the principal mission of the central bank as determining monetary policy objectives aimed at price stability, and ascribes the duties of overseeing payment systems, setting interest rates, and monitoring monetary and exchange rate policies. In this context, it would be appropriate to include financial

BOX 9.3

Legal Infrastructure

The legal framework for the financial system has progressed rapidly in the past five years, expanding the foundation of the legal system, along with institutional arrangements for the implementation of laws. Notable advances include the Law on Commercial Enterprises, the Law on Negotiable Instruments and Payment Transactions, the Law on Secured Transactions, the Law on the Issuance and Trading of Non-Government Securities, the Civil Procedure Code, the Commercial Arbitration Law, and the Law on Insolvency.

However serious gaps, inadequacies, and ambiguities remain:

- The Law on Banks and Financial Institutions lacks adequate provisions on prompt corrective action, safety nets, and bank resolution mechanisms—such as assumption and control and crisis management. This law vests the NBC with powers to provide approvals and exemptions without stating minimum criteria to guide the exercise of discretionary power. Notwithstanding regulations, the law itself is also silent on the NBC's power to oversee and regulate the payment system and credit information system.
- There are conflicts and overlaps in the regulatory laws, and they are uniformly silent on the legal basis for cross-supervisory cooperation. For instance, Article 31 of the Law on the Issuance and Trading of Non-Government Securities provides that no person can conduct a securities business unless licensed by the SECC. Yet Articles 4 and 5 of the Law on Banks and Financial Institutions do permit banks and specialized financial institutions to carry out securities business, including custodial and securities management services. There is no provision in either law on the reconciliation of these two provisions, on consolidated supervision, on the respective roles and responsibilities of the NBC and SECC over bank subsidiaries, or on matters of coordination and cooperation. Until the laws are amended, it is critical for the NBC and SECC to enter into an MoU to deal with these issues. Another serious conflict is the order of priority in the event of insolvency.
- Land is the predominant form of collateral in Cambodia and is preferred by lenders, but despite the importance of this collateral, not all land has been mapped and

titled. Many landowners have so-called soft titles—certificates that are issued and certified by lower authorities (village, commune, or district authorities). The certificates are necessary for the landowners to apply for an official land title, but the costs (a tax of 8 percent on the value of land) and red tape prohibit most landowners from registering the title with the land office. Since financial institutions accept titles issued only at the national level, vast amounts of land end up being untapped as collateral. At the same time, the movable collateral registry established is hardly used, because it is not well known by either lenders or borrowers, and the enforcement of collateral is difficult.

Effective insolvency and creditor rights systems are particularly important in promoting the stability of the financial system. In Cambodia, banks prefer to restructure or roll over loans instead of going to court to recover their debt. Similarly, parties to commercial disputes also seek out-of-court means to settle their disputes. The Insolvency Law—a critical instrument to deal with unproductive and unviable businesses—remains untested, and it is not clear whether the necessary institutional arrangements are in place and the courts have the capacity to handle this important mechanism.

stability as an explicit mandate. The NBC, as the central bank, the monetary authority, and the banking system supervisory authority, is best equipped to discharge this important responsibility. Giving the NBC the necessary legal mandate for maintaining financial stability would help to define oversight roles and provide legal support for relevant oversight duties.

Another gap concerns the ability of the NBC to provide speedy liquidity support and, more broadly, to play an active role in managing liquidity in the system. The NBC can technically provide liquidity to the banking system through three modes: (i) by purchasing or through repurchase agreements (repos) of eligible assets from the banking system; (ii) by granting advances against government or government-guaranteed securities; and (iii) by granting overdrafts against banks' loans. The first two of these facilities are effectively absent, as they are generally dependent on government or central bank securities, which do not exist in Cambodia. The NBC's overdraft facility with loans as collateral has legal and operational shortcomings, which impairs its function as lender of last resort. Key recommendations to the Cambodian authorities include

- making available securities that qualify as eligible collateral for promoting the development of the interbank markets and the central bank liquidity facilities, while exercising caution against moral hazard (as discussed in the previous chapter, this is being achieved by the NBC's granting "collateral" status to fixed deposits placed in it by commercial banks, known as "negotiable certificates of deposit," including government-guaranteed securities);
- establishing legal recognition of the overdraft facility and streamlining its sanctioning process, to have it perform an effective safety net role; and
- empowering the NBC to extend loans, in addition to extending overdrafts, against the collateral of banks' loan portfolios.

A third gap concerns the absence of deposit insurance, an important feature of a financial safety net.[10] The NBC is currently working toward achieving the preconditions for the establishment of deposit insurance, in particular strong supervision. Work has also begun on a feasibility study for a deposit insurance scheme for riel deposits. In the meantime, there is a need to improve the preferential status of depositors' claims vis-à-vis claims of all other creditors, to remove the discrimination between deposits denominated in domestic currency and those denominated in foreign currency; and to consider establishing an improvised and unconventional buffer in each bank to protect depositors' interests.[11]

In the absence of the essential elements of a safety net, the burden of crisis prevention falls squarely on the NBC's supervisory framework in general, and on the prompt corrective action framework in particular.[12] The existing mechanisms need to be strengthened to allow for more effective and timely intervention to ensure financial stability. The main improvements required include: (i) a broader assessment of the financial institution's condition for earlier supervisory response by the NBC; (ii) increased specificity in triggers of responses; (iii) powers to undertake a wider range of supervisory actions; (iv) use of stress test outcomes to influence an early warning system; (v) streamlining and documenting the operational aspects of the prompt corrective action framework; and (vi) enhanced supervisory powers to intervene.

The final "missing" element in the crisis management area is an adequate bank resolution framework. Outside of official administration and liquidation, detailed in the Law on Banking and Financial Institutions, other resolution mechanisms for problem banks are not specified. While the law allows a weak bank to be resolved through liquidation or through an administrator process, the triggers for placing the bank under an administrator and in liquidation are not clearly defined. As highlighted in Box 9.3, the legal framework does not provide for private sector solutions or assisted-bank-resolution options, such as restructuring through mergers and acquisitions, purchase and assumption transactions, and bridge banks.

CONCLUSION

Cambodia's financial system is rapidly evolving, creating new challenges and reinforcing old ones. A robust framework for financial sector oversight is a precondition for a more resilient financial system, one that would enable Cambodia to meet its economic potential. Progress in implementing high-priority FSAP recommendations has been mixed, reflecting in part capacity constraints and the need to forge consensus within the government. On the positive side, the NBC has taken a stricter stance on bank licensing, restructured its banking supervision, and addressed credit risks by introducing a new credit reporting system

[10]Depositors holding deposits denominated in riels rank fifth and depositors holding deposits in other currencies will rank sixth, along with creditors that are banks and financial institutions.

[11]The specific authority should be established in the law with clarifications set forth in regulations.

[12]The prompt corrective action is set forth in a *Prakas*.

coinciding with the launching of a credit information bureau and also by increasing reserve requirement rates.

Still, a full-fledged crisis management framework encompassing all financial supervisors is lacking, while further improving the capacity of banking supervision, both in quantitative and qualitative terms, remains a challenge. At the same time, policy coordination has become even more critical since the launch of the Cambodian stock exchange in April 2012. Also, Cambodia's financial sector is increasingly becoming more interconnected and, hence, idiosyncratic risks may have a systemic impact.

The process of reforms to strengthen supervision faces multidimensional challenges. The first of these has to do with human resources. The relative shortage of qualified technical staff and the lack of capacity may limit the speed of the reform process. There is a scarcity of trained financial professionals, including in the supervisory and regulatory bodies, which can hinder adequate surveillance and timely financial sector supervision. As the financial sector becomes larger and more complex, there is a need to strengthen financial stability oversight to address emerging risks, such as credit expansion, the quality of capital, and shadow banking.

Other important elements that need to be addressed are the establishment of a comprehensive crisis management framework comprising an apex crisis management committee and crisis management team(s); an explicit financial stability mandate for the NBC; a framework for assessing and supervising systemic institutions; crisis management manuals and handbooks; contingency and communication plans; and periodic crisis simulation exercises. A mechanism for dealing with systemic and illiquid or insolvent banks will also help enhance financial stability. Until a supervisory response and prompt corrective action framework are in place, gaps need to be addressed to allow for more effective and timely intervention. Also, work should be initiated toward achieving the preconditions for establishing a deposit insurance scheme.

Index

Page numbers followed by *b, f, n,* or *t* refer to boxed text, figures, footnotes, or tables, respectively.

P

R

S

T